Acclaim for Jan Rutherford's
The Littlest Green Beret
On Self Reliant Leadership

After Jan, I may very well be the next-littlest Green Beret, and maybe that's why he found inspiration from me to cultivate his innate leadership skills in the Airborne and Special Forces. He's proven himself by excelling in both of these elite units, in his civilian profession, and now in leading others to become leaders. I highly recommend this book for developing the leader within all of us.

> –George B. Callahan, CWO4 US Army
> 10th SFG (Retired), and veteran of
> WWII, Korea and Viet Nam

"The Littlest Green Beret" will be a wonderful supplement for leadership students and instructors alike. Through the telling of stories based on Jan's unique experiences and keen observations, this book provides the reader with an engaging overview of what it takes to learn and lead. This book will inspire you to embrace adversity as an opportunity to develop self-reliance for you and those you lead!

> –Sueann Ambron, Ph.D., dean,
> University of Colorado Denver
> Business School

Jan has an important message about leadership...before you can lead others, you have to lead yourself. He tells about his personal journey to self-reliance, and it is a story we can all learn from. Start your journey by reading Jan's book."

> –Paul Spiegelman, Founder and CEO
> of The Beryl Companies, author of
> "Why Is Everyone Smiling?"

Jan Rutherford has written a book that EVERY aspiring leader should read. And every current leader who commits to being the very best for their people should make it a part of their permanent library. Jan's personal journey is one marked by challenge and triumph, of overcoming sometimes monumental odds to persevere ... and to win. "The Littlest Green Beret" is really the true story of a small boy who had the courage to pursue his oversized dreams as he grew to adulthood. There are those who experience adversity and fail, others who simply live their lives hoping to avoid it all together. But there are a very few who so embrace the challenges of life as to make them an integral part of their personal development. There is nothing "little" about this amazing odyssey. Rutherford's gift is born of the insight gained from a lifetime of service, action, and observation. He passes that gift along to his readers. It is a rare gift. This is a rare book.

–Tim Cole, senior pharmaceutical
executive

Having attended the Special Forces Qualification Course (SFQC) with Jan Rutherford, I can attest to his grit and sheer determination to meet challenges and overcome obstacles of any size. "The Littlest Green Beret" sets forth a unique application of hard military lessons to modern business problems. It's filled with real-world anecdotes showing how to apply the principles of self-reliant leadership to everyday business situations. This book should be in every leader's library.

–Andrew W. Bray, Esq., partner, Vernis
& Bowling, Miami, Florida

Too many of our management and leadership books today deal with the outwardly focused processes of leadership and overlook one of the most critical aspects of that subject – self-leadership … "The Littlest Green Beret" uses Jan's unique physical stature as a springboard to challenge each of us to realize that one of the most important parts of good leadership is learning to lead ourselves. Let's face it, very few people really like change or readily recognize the need to change. Jan seeks for us to welcome life's hardships as indicators for the need to change and then deal with making the right changes. I found the book to be very refreshing, and it stimulated me to take a hard look at my own need for change in my life, as well as my views on leadership.

> –Jerry Haney, author, speaker, and
> retired executive

Every proven and aspiring leader should read "The Littlest Green Beret" before passing it on to team members to do the same! This book provides an overview of practical leadership principles for developing self-reliance, creating a personal strategy, and effectively engaging others to create powerful futures.

> –Debra Fine, keynote speaker, trainer,
> and best-selling author of "The Fine Art
> of the Big Talk: How to Win Clients,
> Deliver Great Presentations, and Solve
> Conflicts at Work" (Hyperion)

Rutherford intriguingly articulates a just in time practical, insightful and action packed guide for anyone who wants to be a better leader and a better follower.

> –Kendall Colman, CEO, Colman &
> Company

Such a simple yet powerful book! There are many leadership books out there, but most of them contain so-called "timeless principles" that merely urge managers to use them as checklists for organizational success. I had the unique pleasure of working with Jan many years ago. Although I could see that he was obviously a leader and not a follower, I never took the opportunity to find out what made him tick. What a huge mistake on my part! Jan now shares experiences in his childhood and military experience with us to show us how we can use his life challenges and stories of adversity to extract the hidden leadership skills that lay dormant in all of us. You can't be a good leader without first understanding yourself. I highly recommend this book if you want to enjoy tremendous personal growth and success in all that you do. De Oppresso Liber Jan, from one little Green Beret to another!

–John W. Hedly, Captain, U.S. Army
(Retired)

"The Littlest Green Beret" is more than a book on leadership; it's a book on living life to the fullest and overcoming adversity. Jan Rutherford is a master storyteller who has the ability to teach through example. If you are looking for motivation to change your life or the inspiration to believe that you can ... this is the book for you!

–Greg Giesen, management consultant,
coach, radio talk show host, and author
of the award-winning management
novel, "Mondays At 3"

Jan Rutherford puts us in control of our own path through his powerful and practical look at Self-Reliant Leadership. Extraordinary leadership comes from knowing which questions to ask yourself, and having the courage to answer them and act. Learn these powerful lessons and how to apply them."

–James Downey, Lieutenant Colonel
U.S. Air Force and Vice President,
Global Learning and Organization
Development, CH2M HILL (Retired)

The powerful highlight of this book: the poignant memories of Rutherford's Green Beret activities and how they honed, shaped, and informed his leadership. We all can learn from these lessons!

–Charlotte S. Waisman, Ph.D., author
of "The Leadership Training Activity
Book"

This powerful "little" book packs a tremendous punch for our lives. As we open and pay attention to each moment, for what it is and without judgment, we can truly live OUR principles, be acutely aware, lead meticulously and serve as a role model for kindness and reflection. As we incorporate the lesson in every challenge we see ALL circumstances as positive contributions for growth. Thinking like a leader at all times, even without a leadership title, can create powerful individual and collective differences in the world. Jan's stories are indicative of his understanding of the depth of the human spirit and they demonstrate how determination can lead one forward in the midst of unexpected outcomes. By truly discovering ones values, interaction styles, passions and beliefs we come to know that shifting course is ALWAYS OK. It is a sign that we are paying attention, leading ourselves and functioning as our own authentic source. I have learned a lot from Jan Rutherford over the past few years. He is a living example of humility, compassion, creativity, stamina and resourcefulness because he has opened his eyes to and chosen to learn from each joyous and difficult moment.

–Amy E. Kelsall Ph.D., Academic/
Program Director, University College,
University of Denver, and President of
PeopleWerks

The Littlest Green Beret

On Self-Reliant Leadership

By Jan R. Rutherford, Jr.

Library of Congress Cataloging-in-Publication Data

Rutherford, Jan R. Jr.
     The Littlest Green Beret/Jan R. Rutherford, Jr.
       p. cm.
     ISBN 978-0-9829676-8-3
     1. Green Beret - Military. 2. Self-Reliant - Leadership.
     3. Special Forces - Military.
     4. Independence - Psychology
     5. Success in business - Psychological aspects

Book design by Pylon Publishing LLC

This publication is designed to provide accurate and authoritative information in regard to the subject matter covered. It is sold with the understanding that neither the author nor the publisher is engaged in rendering legal, investment, accounting, or other professional services. If legal advice or other expert assistance is required, the services of a competent professional person should be sought.

Attention: Schools and Businesses

www.pylonpublishing.com

Pylon Publishing books are available at quantity discounts with bulk purchase for educational, business, or sales promotional use. For information go to www.pylonpublishing.com

Dedicated to the West Point Class of 2012

Go n-éirí an bóthar leat

A portion of the proceeds from the sale of this book will be evenly distributed to the following outstanding organizations:

Green Beret Foundation

Special Operations Warrior Foundation

Contents

Acknowledgements

Writing this book involved combing through years of notes, journal entries, and reflecting on what I truly learned from my successes and failures. I have long been an advocate for writing a journal as a means for professional development, and writing this book, where I've attempted to assemble my leadership philosophy through my life stories, has been incredibly enlightening.

The process took much longer than planned and was much harder than I imagined. Much of what I wrote comes from notes and observations made over the past three decades. My aim was to convey that the power to change and improve comes from within, which means asking yourself tough questions.

Before I started writing, I thought I had already asked and answered all the tough questions of myself. Not surprisingly, I constantly questioned whether I had the credibility to write this book because someone once told me the hardest part about teaching leadership is facing your own hypocrisy every time you pontificate.

I have had successes and failures as a practitioner of leadership, but I have never faltered being a student in my quest to understand human motivation and a leader's influence. I also realize that we're all in a constant battle with walking the talk – every day. If you have the requisite humility, you'll see that we're all a work in progress.

I take ownership of my deficiencies, but my successes have come from the support, encouragement, and mentorship of many people for whom I am exceedingly grateful.

My parents taught me the value of hard work, to take pride in any job worth doing, and to never get too big for my britches.

George Callahan helped me understand the true meaning of determination and perseverance.

My son's example of service from an early age showed me the question leaders should constantly ask themselves: "For whose good do I ultimately serve?" My son's love of history, and unrelenting questions about my service caused me to reevaluate what I learned from my past experiences to share with others.

My daughter's own perseverance and ambition to make a difference has always made me reevaluate my own expectations. Though many of the stories contained herein reflect my military experience, and how it's come full circle with my son, my daughter has been the one to challenge me to *walk the talk*. My daughter was the one who asked me about my childhood hopes, dreams, and ambitions – and where and why I had hits and misses. It was my daughter who helped me understand that explaining the "why" when leading is essential to gain unfettered commitment. She has also helped me put more thought into defining my own legacy while striving to be a better man

My wife and soul mate, whose selflessness is saintly, constantly helps me be a better person. Her unwavering faith in me (and gentle nudging) has been a constant inspiration for me to share my stories and pen the chapters that follow. Her encouragement for me to take risks has been a constant source of energy, and my life is infinitely better because of her.

Preface

" "The Littlest Green Beret" represents a small felt hat, my stature, and all those seemingly insurmountable goals. We all face adversity amidst physical, mental, and emotional challenges, and this book is about becoming self-reliant in terms of creating a powerful future. It can also become your battle plan for addressing life's challenges and the key to unlocking the leader within you.

Through my own stories of adversity, I will convey how leadership development can occur every day if you're observant, reflective, and determined. This book provides an overview of practical leadership principles for managing oneself, creating a personal strategy, and effectively engaging others to assist you with your own developmental objectives.

By exploring what effective leaders actually do and how they do it, you will learn the principles of personal effectiveness and how visionary leadership can develop and inspire people to achieve more than they thought they could. Leadership can be an illusion of control, but changing your perspective on everyday experiences can provide inspirational learning opportunities for personal growth and development.

Forward

Dr. Alexander Bracken,
President Emeritus,
University of Colorado

L ife has numerous challenges, many which we can do nothing about, like being physically short. Achieving self-reliant leadership is about over-coming these challenges and doing more than you ever thought possible.

No-one has the "formula" for optimal leadership. There is no perfect template. What we all have, however, is the opportunity to work on developing our interpersonal relations which is at the heart of effective leadership says Rutherford. Overcoming the stigma and associated limitations of being short or whatever limitation one may have is part of the self-reliant aspect Rutherford talks about. Setbacks and even failures are valuable learning and growth experiences. How to learn from them is the crux of the leadership issue according to Rutherford.

Each chapter of the book concludes with a take away – a leadership trait or example of outstanding leadership that we can focus our attention on and practice ourselves, thereby becoming more effective in our own self-reliant leadership. Bottom line, we desperately need excellent leadership. Examples abound of ineffective leadership: translate – brutal, fraudulent or despicable behavior exhibited in "leaders." Jan Rutherford provides a pathway for leadership growth that is exemplary and positive, inspiring and trustworthy, and influential and impactful.

This book does not give you a "10 point" plan to go through and immediately be declared a good leader. What this book does provide is guidance that will help you develop a pathway to learn from your own experiences on how to build effective leadership skills. Coming from one who has witnessed leadership at a very high level, taught leadership to MBA students, and, most significantly, exhibited leadership throughout his business career, Jan Rutherford delivers a powerful approach to becoming the leader that you aspire to be and that we most definitely need.

Introduction – You and This Book

self-re·li·ant   [self-ri-lahy-uhnt, self-]

–adjective
relying on oneself or on one's own powers, resources, etc.

–Synonyms
independent, assured, enterprising, resolute, capable.

"The Little Green Beret" represents a small felt hat, my stature, and a tangible object representing all those seemingly insurmountable goals. We all face adversity amidst physical, mental, and emotional challenges, and this book is about becoming self-reliant in terms of creating a powerful future. It can also become your battle plan for addressing life's challenges and the key to unlocking the leader within you.

I'm not sure whether I am actually the smallest man to ever complete the Special Forces Qualification Course and earn the Army's coveted green beret, but I was the littlest person I came across during my nine years of service. The adversity I faced early on made a significant impression on my perspective about *what makes a leader*.

Back then, at 5 feet 4½ inches, I was 114 pounds of

stubbornness with a huge drive to prove my father, my sister, and one very loud and condescending drill sergeant that they were wrong – that I could make it in the Army, and even Special Forces.

That was 1979. I remember that I wanted to get squared away so I could save money, go to college, and become self-reliant. My goal in this book is much grander: I want to help leaders develop their own self-reliance to create powerful futures because leadership development can occur every day if you're observant, reflective, and determined. **Self-Reliant Leadership is synonymous with knowing which questions to ask yourself and having the courage to answer them and act.**

Leadership can be an illusion of control, but changing your perspective on everyday experiences can provide inspirational learning opportunities for personal growth and development. My hope is the stories contained within this book will help you get the most out of your own personal approach to leadership – that is, achieve high levels of sustainable personal effectiveness; communicate more clearly and powerfully; and inspire others to *willingly* follow you in support of your efforts to make a difference.

What questions should you routinely ask yourself? On a daily basis, what steps should you take to find personal success in your life's work? ***Do you know your life's work?*** Some say it's the place where your passion and others' needs intersect. I believe a key determinant of success is whether you can rely on yourself for self-coaching. However, self-reliant leadership is dependent on achieving a balance between independence and the interdependence of working
with others to accelerate your own personal growth and development.

Self-reliance and Leadership may seem to be contradictory notions, but there are three mutually supporting concepts. Leadership requires **Self-awareness**. Leaders understand their strengths and shortcomings and how those traits affect their ability to create willing followers. The second is **Selflessness**. A leader needs to have a steadfast passion for serving others, and that requires putting others first. Lastly, **Self-reliance** is essential because leading means being out front, and there are more naysayers than supporters when trailblazing. Self-Reliant Leaders believe in leading by example to develop followers who have initiative, persistence, and determination. **Self-awareness, Selflessness,** and **Self-reliance** are the three character traits that are the lifelong pursuit of effective and outstanding leaders.

I have always been fascinated by what separates the ordinary from the extraordinary. Most of us are average – by definition, of course. Why do some of us excel beyond all expectations while many just exist and subsist? As I reflect back on my experiences, I remember acutely how miserable it was being so small – not average. In hindsight, I now know that it was actually a tremendous gift. It helped me become an astute observer of human behavior, prejudice, and a detector of authenticity. Overcoming an early adversity was a character builder, and obtaining the green beret was validation that anything is possible if you want it bad enough. I certainly would not be who I am today had it not been for the trials and tribulations that accompanied my own crucibles.

I also believe the key component that separates effective leaders from average leaders is the discipline to sacrifice and the ability to endure hardship to strengthen one's resolve. In other words, leaders are comfortable with being uncomfortable because they know every life event thrown their way can be a tremendous learning experience. The successful people I have known have a distinct ability to positively inspire and influence others to be their best – that is, *To Lead.* I believe the ability to create *willing followers* is what defines effective teachers as well. If you think about it, most people who have had a positive influence on your life have taught you something –

or rather, helped you see something you otherwise wouldn't: something about yourself.

I have had roles as both a leader and a follower. What most interested me about the Army Special Forces was the self-reliant aspect of survival; the risk taking affiliated with jumping out of perfectly good airplanes; preparing for worldwide deployment at a moment's notice; the opportunity to help others as the Army's best-trained medic; being part of an elite team with a mission to *free the oppressed*; and the prospect of seeing firsthand why some people succeed as leaders while others flounder, regardless of the rank that adorns their collar. Observing the twelve men on an "A" team (an elite team inside Special Forces) during a mission is a fascinating leadership laboratory and one I was able to experience while still a teenager.

I do not believe any book can teach you how to be an effective leader – including this one. Moreover, I don't think knowing every aspect of every leadership theory will make you an effective leader. It comes down to the application of interpersonal relations as the art of leadership. No blueprint or paint-by-numbers scheme can cover the contingencies for the infinite combination of situations, people, and motivations.

What I can offer you is a way to turn yourself into a living laboratory by empowering *yourself* to start a lifelong journey of observation, persistence, humility, and a disciplined approach to trial and error (with lots of emphasis on the errors because that is where the learning always takes place).

You have watched people lead your whole life – your parents, teachers, coaches, and bosses. Some did it well, and some had gaping holes in their technique and effectiveness. Collectively, they have influenced the way you perceive, process, make decisions, and perform as a leader.

I have had the great fortune of meeting a few notable leaders, which provided me the opportunity to learn something about myself, and more importantly, my impact on others.

Oft quoted, but *when you are ready to learn, the teacher will appear.*

Leaders are molded from the experiences of their life, and great leaders learn from these experiences (more from the setbacks) at a faster rate than others. I suspect that great leaders intuitively know how to pick organizations and roles where their interests, skills, experiences, and values are aligned with their passions.

This book is about learning how to learn – knowing yourself, learning from your mistakes, learning from observation, questioning, and using inevitable situations that will test your mettle while forcing adjustments to create rich learning experiences. This book is not a step-by-step list for various leadership challenges, but a guide to help you learn about becoming self-reliant to take charge of your own personal growth as a leader in order to create a powerful future. You will have to adapt and change. Try it. There are plenty of people who desperately need you.

Chapter 1 – Self-Reliance

The greatest achievement of the human spirit is to live up to one's opportunities and make the most of one's resources.
–Marquis De Vauvenargues[1]

The woods have always called to me, and when I was a boy in Naples, Florida, I desperately wanted two things. One was to live in the woods all by myself for a year like the main fictional character in "My Side of the Mountain." This book by Jean George absolutely spoke to me. Sam Gribley was a 13-year-old boy from a large family, living in New York City. He convinced his parents to let him live in the Catskill Mountains for one year where he took up residence in a hollowed-out tree, trained a falcon to hunt small prey, and kept a journal of his trials and tribulations.

Every year, I would ask my parents if I could live in the Everglades near my home for a year (it never occurred to me that I was reading fiction). My parents repeatedly said no; they wouldn't even let me try it for a few short weeks.

But on weekends, the parental strings were looser, and

---

1 Luc de Clapiers, marquis de Vauvenargues (1715-1747) was a French moralist whose belief in the individual's capacity for goodness played a part in the shift of opinion away from the pessimistic view of human nature elaborated by 17th century thinkers. Source: Encyclopedia Britannica Online, 2006.

my friends and I would head to the woods with only bare essentials. We always managed to subsist in the pristine pine forest and mangrove swamps that existed around Naples in the early 1970s. We'd catch our own bait by using treble hooks to snag mullet and needlefish, or catch fiddler crabs or snails along the seawalls. We used the bait to catch snapper and anything that was big enough to actually produce a filet. I'd take my twenty-gauge junior-model shotgun, and we'd shoot rabbits and quail to roast on a stick over a fire built from sappy pines that produced a ton of smoke. We would look for edible plants to eat, like prickly pear cacti. We usually took sleeping bags, but the miserable choice meant sweltering inside or getting devoured by mosquitoes – or both! The obvious solution was to get big Swisher Sweets cigars and smoke out the mosquitoes. We thought everything we did was self-sufficient and very composed.

This was where I began to learn and appreciate the concept of self-reliance while building my own self-confidence.

The other thing I desperately wanted as a boy was to play "Pop Warner football" – with shoulder pads, rugged helmets, and enthusiastic coaches. I had always loved team sports, especially football, though I was not particularly fast. Because of my small stature, I tried exceptionally hard to show how tough I was, and I had a naturally competitive spirit. Despite my parents' stern warning not to try out for the football team, I would go out every year. The coach would pick me up, set me down, grin at the other coaches, and tell me I was too little. The coach's rejection included an explanation that it was for my own good so I wouldn't get hurt. I would go home and cry with embarrassment. Looking back, I know my parents wanted to protect me from the inevitable dejection.

When I turned 13, in my stubbornness, I again went to try out. The coach again picked me up underneath my arms so that my eyes met his and announced that I would probably weigh the requisite amount of 65 pounds – if I were fully dressed out in football pads. Finally, I was able to play Pop Warner football! I enjoyed pushing myself physically and loved the concept of a team working together to accomplish its goals. I almost made the traveling team, but I wasn't quick enough compared to the others trying out for the running back position.

The next year was high school; I weighed about the same and realized, through simple physics, there was no way I was going to play high school football with kids who weighed two to three times more than me. It never occurred to me there might be individual sports like swimming or cross-country running where size is less of a factor. Part of the Southern culture then, and arguably still, made it seem that football was the only sport that mattered.

I was always an above-average student, but we moved away from my beloved woods while I was in ninth grade, and I lost my academic focus. All I cared about in high school was playing the drums and chasing girls. While in high school, I worked at assorted labor-intensive jobs more than thirty hours per week and always thought I would attend college. The menial jobs all involved some sort of cleaning of disgusting places – mechanic bays at a car dealership, the ban saws at a meat market, or bathrooms at a fast-food restaurant. This inspired me to seek a career where I could use my head instead of my hands.

During the fall of my senior year, I received a letter from the University of Florida music department saying I had been accepted into their program. When I shared this fine news with my parents, their reply was, "Did you get a scholarship with that? We don't have the money to send you to college." In fairness, I think they believed all I would do in college was party, and they were probably right. As a result, I decided I would still pursue a career in music, only through different means.

I began looking at joining the Army. Deep down, I knew I needed to be more disciplined – and I needed money for college. The structured discipline combined with time in the outdoors appealed to me. In my senior class of more than 800 students, there was only one other person who enlisted in the military. There was no draft, no war, and memories of Vietnam were fresh. Bright kids did not join the Army, and young men who barely weighed 100 pounds did not sign up for Special Forces. The recruiters in 1978 were more than happy to talk with people who scored high on their aptitude test. Many of those joining at that time had been directed by a judge or magistrate.

The recruiter quickly arranged an audition for me at Fort McPherson, Georgia, with one of the Army's bands. Somehow, during that trip (and my first commercial airline flight), I realized I was not talented enough to make a living as a career musician but thought the Army might be a good start for a lost soul like me. Plus, if I contributed $75 per month to a college fund, the Army would contribute $150, for a three-year total of $8,100 (the GI Bill did not exist at the time). The flight home was the closest I would ever come to having a real epiphany.

When I landed in Miami, I was met by my recruiter, Sergeant First Class Kyle Fleenor, a Vietnam veteran from Tennessee. I told him I was not going to pursue music in the Army. He looked completely depressed until I said I wanted to learn about the Army's toughest and most comprehensive medical program. And I said one more thing: "If I could jump out of planes, that would be pretty cool!"

Sergeant Fleenor immediately suggested that the Army's hardest medic program was in Special Forces. I told him I was not interested in the military police. He laughed and said, "Special Forces is not the MPs, it's the Green Berets!"

He handed me a brochure that showed a camouflaged, square-jawed soldier with huge biceps paddling a rubber boat while wearing the coveted green beret. At the time, I literally weighed 101 pounds and still stood 5 feet 4½ inches tall. I told Kyle there was no way I could make it. I had quit playing sports in high school out of frustration with being so little because if I couldn't play football, why bother? Kyle looked me dead in the eyes and said, "Sure you can. You can make it." Sergeant Fleenor's seven words completely changed my life's direction. I didn't know it at the time, but that was the moment when I embraced the idea that I could do anything I set my mind to.

I tried to join the Army while still a senior in high school, but the physician at the recruiting station told me I had to weigh at least 103 pounds to get a waiver to jump out of planes. I immediately started running, lifting weights, and drinking banana milkshakes with Joe Weider's supplement for weight gain to meet the minimum standards. A few months later, I weighed 109 pounds and was able to join the Army in a delayed-entry program. My parents had to sign for me because I was only 17 years old.

The rest of my senior year of high school was focused on preparation for basic training that would begin two weeks after graduation. To prepare for a grueling summer boot camp in South Carolina, I ran in the heat of the day in South Miami where I would get drenched with sweat while gnats and mosquitoes stuck to the skin on my face, arms, and chest. I eventually felt ready for the unknown. One day, I was in my room listening to "The Ballad of the Green Berets" on a record. This was before you could easily transport your music while running, and I thought the ballad got me psyched up for my runs. My sister interrupted my meditative state, looked at the record player, and said harshly, "What are you going to do when you fail?"

Though I had my doubts, I never seriously entertained the idea of not making it. I didn't have a Plan B. My dad soon followed up on this theme with a bet of $1,000 that I wouldn't make it through basic training and $10,000 that I wouldn't earn the green beret. I didn't know it at the time, but both of those "negative motivators" would serve me well when the going got much tougher.

I also had two very positive influences affecting me at the same time. One was Kyle Fleenor, the recruiter previously mentioned, who would run with me a few times a week and offer lots of encouragement. Kyle had been awarded the Purple Heart for a wound he suffered in his posterior while in Vietnam, and he had a funny story like the fictional Forrest Gump.

The other person was George Callahan, a neighbor who was rumored to have been a Navy admiral. In fact, he was a decorated combat veteran of World War II, Korea, Vietnam, and was a former Army Special Forces soldier. He went through paratrooper and Special Forces training at the unprecedented age of 40. He was the complete opposite of what you would expect a Special Forces soldier to look like: small in stature, soft-spoken, kind, polite. He also had a delightful crooked smile that was only enhanced by penetrating blue eyes. George had one daughter and no sons. When he learned that I had enlisted and signed up for Special Forces training, he invited me into his home where he told war stories and showed me military memorabilia and old photographs. George was positive, optimistic, immensely inspiring, and completely encouraging.

I would draw on all four of these people – my sister, father, a recruiter, and an old veteran – to make it through the training that at times seemed unbearable. Part of what I learned in the training is that in addition to sacrifice, there is a fair amount of suffering required. This suffering had everything to do with self-discipline, but I did not grasp this connection until some years later. When I was 17, I had not yet learned how to suffer. George helped me with this before I left home.

One day before I left for boot camp, I eagerly asked my mentor George for advice that would help me in my training. He said he had only two bits of advice: "Choose your friends carefully. You need to work with everyone, but not everyone has to be your friend."

This was great advice that has served me well, but the concept did not take hold completely until years later. The other counsel offered was, "Take the bad times day by day. If it's really bad, take it hour by hour. If it's really, really bad, take it moment by moment."

That particular advice sunk in soon after my military indoctrination began. One day I was crouched under a mildewed rubber poncho in a cold rainstorm, hungry and sleep deprived. I knew that I would soon be called on to lead a patrol and expend energy I didn't think I had in reserve – and that a noncommissioned officer would evaluate my performance. It was those moments when I was wet, cold, tired, and hungry that I wanted to quit. I heard echoes of my sister and father suggesting I would fail. How I wanted to prove them wrong.

I remember when a drill sergeant mockingly asked my basic training platoon, "Who among you is headed for Special Forces training?"

I was the only one who raised a hand. He looked at my frame (I was up to 114 pounds) and told the platoon that I wouldn't make it – the backpack I would be required to carry would weigh more than me. Everyone in the platoon joined in with the drill sergeant's laughter.

I earned the Army's green beret on November 12, 1980. I was barely 19 years old. My parents were beaming at the graduation ceremony, and I was so glad they drove from Miami to Fort Bragg to see me. I didn't receive the $10,000 from my dad, but George gave me one of his cherished old berets, which was a monumental honor. He also had one more piece of advice: "As hard as the past eighteen months of training have been, that is not the hardest thing you will face." I thought he was talking about the physical toll, but I have since learned that his comment had a much broader context.

For my first assignment, I was selected to become an instructor for the Special Forces school (part of the John F. Kennedy Special Warfare Center and School – the Army's Special Operations University). I was immediately made an acting sergeant, even though I was only a private first class with eighteen months of service. So I had my beret, sergeant stripes, and by and large felt pretty darn good about myself.

About a year later, an interesting thing happened. The drill sergeant who laughed at the prospect of me making it through Special Forces training due to my size was now one of the new students in the Special Forces Qualification Course – a candidate vying to earn a green beret. Two things happened when a student quit: Trucks would be called to take the student back to Fort Bragg from the camp and "Another One Bites the Dust" by the rock band Queen would play over the loudspeakers. The former drill sergeant became one of those who quit. I saw him sitting dejectedly while waiting for the truck, and I approached him. I asked if he remembered me. He just looked up at me, shook his head no, and put his head back down without saying a word. I didn't say a word either. I didn't need to. There are plenty of things I am not proud of, but I will always be glad I didn't say anything to that former drill sergeant to make him feel worse. It wouldn't have made me feel better, and I know quitting once makes quitting again easier, and that regret is hard enough to live with.

It's fascinating to study why some lead and some follow – and I've had roles in both capacities.

It takes the same self-reliance to survive in the brush as it does to survive in a position of leadership. A person needs the same ability to take risks if he or she is jumping out of a plane or taking an organization in a radical new direction.

To become a leader who inspires others to greatness (or at least to do their best), you need to turn yourself into a "living laboratory." Everyone is molded by his or her experiences – including and especially by his or her mistakes. Great leaders learn the lessons from their experiences faster than other people.

You may have heard the suggestion that you should "dress" for the position you want. My suggestion to you is that you start your career in leadership by thinking like a leader no matter what your position.

Start now to process those daily "people" observations into lessons you can use about how you affect and influence others.

Don't be one of those people who can't admit to themselves or others that they make mistakes. Haven't we all seen enough giants brought down because of that hubris? Embrace those mistakes as just lessons that are important for you to learn. Throughout this book, we'll talk about how to take your mistakes, process them through your mind and heart, and then make "course corrections."

Even under the best of circumstances, your current trajectory will require periodic adjustments. During land navigation training in the Army, I learned that even the tiniest error with a compass becomes more significant the farther you travel. We learned to focus on a point that we could see, such as a large knot on a tree, and make sure we had the correct heading to that particular point. We would then do the same thing over again once we got to each marker. A five-mile trip through the underbrush might really be twenty short trips with constant course corrections.

This same principle applies to your own leadership development: Your journey will include many measurements with plenty of course corrections that sometimes involve going back a few steps to ensure the path is correct. Sometimes we encountered muddy swamps where we had to decide if it was easier to go through slowly and get muddy or go around and risk getting disoriented (we never used the word "lost").

Often, we ask others for their secrets to success. But this means we will continue to avoid creating and answering the tough questions for ourselves. I know so few people who can watch someone make a mistake and learn as much as if they had made it themselves.

A rule that many of us have learned – and that I guarantee you'll learn for yourself if you haven't already – is you can't change others. It would certainly be easier if we could stroll through life modifying this person and that person to our own satisfaction and standards. A little more eloquence here! A lot more intelligence there! Even though most people would nod and agree that yes, we know we can't change others, almost nobody believes it. People spend tons of energy that could be used in other places while trying to remake their spouse, parents, children, and co-workers. We'll talk about instigating change in great detail in chapter nine.

In order to make a difference, you must constantly adapt and change ... **constantly change** ... not because of outside demands, but because your internal laboratory will be telling you "This doesn't work" or "This works much better" and "This is the way a great leader would act."

Use the **Take Away** at the end of each chapter to generate ideas. Start coaching yourself by setting reasonable and achievable short-term goals so your ability to succeed will not be dependent on bosses, schools, professors, motivational speakers, or even this book. Your success will depend on you – the self-reliant leader.

Take Away

I believe that **experience** is the best teacher. Seventy percent of success is really about showing up, and that idea encompasses whole worlds of thought. You show up and bring your body and your mind and your spirit. You show up with your mind as open as you can get it. You show up at places where you'll have new experiences that are related to your goals; otherwise, you'll miss key learning opportunities. Remember, you want to grow your wisdom and strength as quickly as you can.

To spend your time in the right place, you will need to **sacrifice** something. That shouldn't be a scary word. Sometimes you have to forego immediate gratification for later gain. Think about the diet and exercise mantra: Eat less, exercise more. If you are not exercising at all and decide to exercise one hour per day, you will have to give up that one hour from something you currently do. Sacrifice that one hour per day for something that may not be as pleasant but helps you obtain a long-term goal – health. You can count on days when your mind tries to talk you out of exercising with an irrational argument taking place between your ears. Think about what you will stop doing, what you will start doing, and what you will keep doing in the context of your goals.

You must stay focused, and to do that you need unwavering **discipline** to persevere. Embrace obstacles and adversity, as they can serve as a source of strength and personal growth. Best-selling author Gail Sheehy wrote a book called "Pathfinders" after interviewing people who had made a difference in the world. She said she expected to find they were born to the right parents, went to the right schools, and made the right choices of mate, work, and environment. In 100 percent of the cases, that was untrue. The one thing all these people had in common was that they had experienced a "dark night of the soul," some trauma, some emotional or physical challenge, where they had to develop the character and fortitude to come out the other side. They took adversity and let it shape them. They in turn helped shape the world.

Leverage your time and enhance your powers of observation to gain insights that accelerate your own personal growth and development. Think like a descriptive writer. Observe everything and make mental notes: Connect the dots, see complementary and opposing forces, make correlations, and draw conclusions (even if you're wrong, you'll learn from it!). Make new behaviors a **habit** that will strengthen your character to make a difference in the lives of others.

But first, you have to know yourself. *Self-Reliant Leadership is synonymous with knowing which questions to ask yourself and having the courage to answer them and act.*

What was the earliest adversity you faced, and how has it affected your life?

Who are the leaders you admire, and what are the traits that make them effective?

What does self-reliance mean to you?

Only very few civilized persons are capable of existing without reliance on others or are even capable of coming to an independent opinion.

                 –Sigmund Freud, father of
                 psychoanalysis

Chapter 2 – Crucibles

"Without pain, there's no adversity. Without adversity, no challenge. Without challenge, no improvement. No improvement, no sense of accomplishment and no deep-down joy."

–Scott Martin, sports columnist

Effective leaders are known for having an inquisitive mind and an insatiable appetite for learning about what makes people tick. A crucible provides the opportunity to reflect on what you see, hear, and process – especially during the tests of adversity. Much has been written about the "crucibles of leadership," and leadership expert Warren Bennis' notable observation was that leaders are tempered in the crucible of experience.

We made two major moves when I was a kid. We left Rochester, New York, for Naples, Florida, when I was 9 years old. When I was 14, we left Naples on the rural (at the time) west coast of Florida for Homestead on the urban east coast. Both moves came at difficult and awkward transitional ages. When we moved to Florida in 1971, the Southern culture was quite different from Upstate New York. Yes, South Florida was "Southern" once upon a time! I started kindergarten when I was 4, so I was not only small, but always young for my grade. In middle school, as everyone knows, kids can be cruel. Kids teased me and called me munchkin, peanut, shrimp, and shorty, and ever since I have hated nicknames.

One day while sitting on the edge of the school's track during lunch, a bunch of kids grabbed me from behind, picked me up, and threw me in the cafeteria's dumpster. Instead of being covered with food, I was covered in pencil shavings and had some pencil lead poked under the skin on my arms and hands. I was humiliated, and I was mostly frustrated that I had no control over the situation. I couldn't beat up the kids – partly because I didn't see who had picked me up from behind and mostly because I was so little. I also couldn't turn them in – I'd surely suffer a worse fate. My mom unceremoniously interrogated me upon viewing my disheveled appearance, but I couldn't reveal my tormenters even if I wanted to. My mom forced a meeting with the principal out of concern for my safety, and he assured her that he would look after me. That was the last thing I wanted – to be coddled. To make matters worse, he told me that he was small for his age in middle school, but I didn't believe him and saw him as manipulative.

I decided then and there that I would show the kids that I wasn't just some smaller version of them. Despite society's obsession with a child's growth, as if it's controllable, I'd have to use my wits to build credibility as a "normal" kid. I decided the best way was to expressly offer my opinions and observations on daily events of student life. I surely didn't understand the concept at the time, but I was making a conscious decision to become a *fake extrovert* to exert more control over my own fate and put forth some semblance of self-control and influence over others. A new nickname was added to the kids' repertoire to describe me – "brain." I still disliked the label, but found this one more palatable. The outcome of my own forced personality transition was that I was becoming an astute observer of human behavior. If it was to be, it was up to me. If

I indeed took control of how I responded to the environment, I could change, enhance, or temper a given situation, and that meant I had to be proactive and goal oriented. The sharper the goal in my mind's eye, the more optimistic I became at achieving the goal. And when I achieved small wins, I became more optimistic about accomplishing goals that were more ambitious.

I have had about twenty major moves in my life, and during each move, I never considered how ridiculous the perpetual motion might have seemed to others. I didn't realize it at the time, but as a result of all the moves, I was developing plenty of adaptive skills. In hindsight, I truly wonder what I was thinking! What propelled me on each subsequent move was the promise of getting closer to my overarching goal of a more fulfilling life. Each move was made with the express objective to improve my life by learning new skills, taking on new responsibilities, and challenging myself. In each case there was a potential to fail, but also the opportunity and possibility to grow and thrive. The optimist in me was always confident my sacrifices and calculated risks would pay future dividends.

I don't believe one has to make twenty physical moves to achieve big goals, but I do believe one has to make numerous mental and emotional shifts to get where one wants to be. I'm not sure how you make any sort of move without being self-assured that things will work out; otherwise, you'd have every incentive to stay comfortable and risk averse. Whether you succeed or fail, you have to learn, and that alone will help you advance toward your long-term goals if you're willing to take even a slightly different tact on subsequent efforts. "Nothing ventured, nothing gained" may be trite, but there is wisdom in that maxim to keep in mind as you weigh options for the path you choose.

Because I started being perceived as "brainy," my teacher in seventh grade encouraged me to enter a speech contest. She described the experience as one of growth and enlightenment, and though it scared me to death, I relished the challenge. The subject for all competitors was "I'm Just One." There was no guidance, other than the speech was to be five minutes long and had to be memorized. I wish I still had the speech my dad helped me write because the only thing I remember is that my opening line was, "I'm just one," and then I posed a question and referenced one of the Roosevelt presidents (probably Theodore because he was the self-reliant outdoorsman).

My five-minute speech was mediocre at best, and my gestures were forced and unnatural. In my mind I had great inflection, but I'm sure I was monotone and shaky because I forgot my words halfway through. I became completely preoccupied with my hands behind my back, thinking that if I squeezed them hard enough, I would be able to pick up where I stopped. At the time, I thought I was learning about public speaking, but the real lesson was in learning that "I'm Just One" is a fantastic starting point to learn about one's character and purpose. There is no better place to start learning than asking yourself who you are, why you're here, and what you can do as one person to make a difference in the lives of others.

To this day, that speech taught me to listen to that little voice that says, "You can do it – just listen to yourself – you can make a difference!" That crucible, the speech I remembered, the speech I forgot, taught me that adversity incubates awareness and growth.

It was also in seventh grade that I started earning money and interacting with adults. I got the coveted paper route that covered Vanderbilt Beach in Naples. The job required me to fold papers after school, which took about half an hour, followed by delivering papers to about 100 houses. It was at least a two-hour commitment per day after school. At the time, the paved road along Vanderbilt Beach didn't go through the entire way, so riding my bike required walking my bike as well. In addition, afternoon rainstorms were pretty reliable, so most of the time the route involved a drenching. If I didn't keep the papers dry, customers would complain and my pay would get docked. The job taught me a few things at that young age. Stamina is important. You've got to give it your all even when you're tired. Hard work pays dividends, as I was able to win a sleeping bag by being selected as the best paperboy at one point (a prized possession for a boy who wanted to live in the woods). It was also a job that allowed me plenty of time to think and contemplate my future. I learned that if I sacrificed free time and worked hard, it would result in good things. I learned to take pride in a job well done, and that hard work eventually gets noticed.

Take Away

The examples cited above have a couple of things in common. There was adversity, doubt, and time to reflect. Understanding how you'll react to adversity helps to remove doubt while focusing on short-term sacrifices for long-term gains. There's nothing like a crucible to help you understand what you're good at and what you enjoy (i.e., your passion). My boyhood experiences certainly shaped my decision to join the Army, seek mighty challenges, and banish the word "can't." There are a number of resources available for self-discovery, and a first-rate and down-to-earth starting point is to write out your own beliefs and core values. Values are the foundation upon which a leadership philosophy is honed that fits your interests, skills, and expectations. To help ignite your creativity, here's how other authors have defined leadership:

Peter Drucker: "The only definition of a leader is someone who has followers."

John C. Maxwell: "Leadership is influence – nothing more, nothing less."

Warren Bennis: "Leadership is a function of knowing yourself, having a vision that is well communicated, building trust among colleagues, and taking effective action to realize your own leadership potential."

John W. Gardner: "Leadership is the process of persuasion and example by which an individual (or leadership team) induces a group to take action that is in accord with the leader's purpose, or the shared purposes of all."

Self-Reliant Leadership is synonymous with knowing which questions to ask yourself and having the courage to answer them and act.

Whether you are looking for concepts to jump-start an idea or because you are looking for motivation or inspiration, consider three of the most important questions you can ask when facing an obstacle or trying to advance your objectives through others:

Where am I?

Where do I want to be?

How will I get there?

Where am I? is a broad question that requires a great deal of introspection. This is difficult because it requires you to be painfully honest with yourself – honest about your strengths and honest about parts of your character that may be holding you back. Who knows you better than you ultimately know yourself?

Where do you want to be? helps you focus your purpose. What does success look like and feel like to you? It is fine to dream big, but the important thing is to dream. It is critical that you decide your life's passion, because creating a vision will mean making a difference in the lives of others. How you achieve your goals will have a great deal to do with how you respond to your environment – that is, *your attitude*. People follow optimists and those who provide hope. You only need to look at political elections to see that pessimists and those who flip-flop on issues are seen as weak and seldom win. Throughout history, people have followed leaders who were sure of themselves, and such is the need to believe that good leaders bring hope for a better outcome and future.

How will I get there? What are the details of *how* you will make a difference? The difference you want to make in this world requires some degree of influence with others. Think of the difference you will make as a form of service. How will you get to the place you so eloquently described for your team? How will you track your progress in order to adjust for optimal performance? Are you making progress towards this goal in your daily activities – i.e., how you spend your time?

The things we know best are the things we haven't been taught.

–Marquis De Vauvenargues, French moralist

Chapter 3 – Coaching

A man is what he thinks about all day long.
           –Ralph Waldo Emerson, lecturer,
           essayist and poet

Teaching and coaching can be interchangeable when the objective is to guide people to the source of their own power, and coaching is a fundamental skill of effective leaders.

Growing up, my neighbor was a good old boy from Alabama and a former Marine. Jerry Snell was slightly younger than my parents, and he was still in great physical shape. He was a wicked-fast runner, a quiet, brooding type who could best be described as a man's man. I'm not sure why he left the Marines, but I remember a version of a story where he "accidentally" fired a pistol on a ship. He had his own successful business building homes with his father, and it seemed like he knew how to build anything and fix everything. Jerry took me under his wing and taught me how to hunt and fish and was the first person who inspired in me the concept of self-reliance: You have to be squared away first before you can ask anything of anyone else.

Jerry was a certified scuba diver, and he taught me how

to use his scuba tanks to clean his pool (*sort of like Tom Sawyer getting his friends to whitewash his picket fence*). He also thought it was his responsibility to simulate the Navy's celebrated SEAL training. Jerry was ruthless in dunking me to a near drowning, but I loved the attention and thought his version of wrestling made me tough. He was also the guy who encouraged me to take risks, like diving into the pool from his roof! When we hunted in the Everglades, I was amazed he trusted me enough to carry a rifle – as an 11 year old! He also told me I could shoot game without checking with him first. This was a huge deal to me, and I remember feeling like a man when I quietly followed him through the dense swamp in chest-deep water. If I followed him too closely, he would be sure to let a branch swing back and hit me right in the face. He would then sternly caution, "Don't follow too close, boy." His coaching style definitely didn't involve coddling, and I'm sure he was grinning when he knew I couldn't see him.

It amazed me that Jerry knew the woods and swamp so intimately. One time when we were out all day in waist-deep water with water moccasins and alligators all around, he said, "Now take us back to camp."

I protested and said, "I can't do that – I've just been following you and watching for snakes."

He said, "Well, it's going to be a long night then."

I led us back to camp eventually, and we got in as darkness descended. Instead of congratulating me on my land navigation skills, Jerry said, "Next time, pay attention. What would you do if something happened to me?"

He had a point – actually, he had two points: I needed to rely on myself, and I needed to think about contingencies for others. Adapt, conserve energy, and keep it simple. Leadership defined.

We moved away when I was 14, but Jerry had an impact on me for the rest of my life. As I was growing up and trying to figure out what sort of man I wanted to be, I would often think of Jerry. Jerry was an inspiration for me to develop my own sense of self-reliance.

Self-awareness and self-discipline are the essence of self-coaching. They allow you to draw on your own power and resources to minimize weaknesses while leveraging strengths to exploit opportunities towards the achievement of goals. Leadership can be an illusion of control, but vigorously embracing everyday experiences can provide inspirational learning opportunities for personal growth and development. The ability to operate and sustain a high level of energy is a key determinant of success. At the same time, the knack to adapt to changing situations and opportunities – possessing flexibility – is also vital. The common theme is discipline from within.

I believe you see peoples' true character when they're wet, cold, tired, and hungry. In other words, when people face adversity, you see different things in them than when they're relatively comfortable. *No pain, no change.* Jerry instinctively knew that he could see and shape me better when things were difficult. I wasn't often cold in the Everglades, but I was always wet and tired! Through Jerry, part of my very identity was forged through perpetual motion, fitness, and the solitude of the wilderness.

Whether you're trudging through a swamp, climbing a mountain, or dealing with difficult people, adversity serves as a source of strength, resolve, and optimism. Adversity is a coaching crucible, and every crisis reveals character in ways status quo cannot. If effective coaching consists in large part to creating a compelling vision, then it makes sense that a compelling vision is hopeful and optimistic. The human spirit has always endured because "hope springs eternal," and one certainly cannot effectively lead as a pessimist. In a crisis, it's a good rule of thumb to "control the *controllables*" because you cannot plan for every external variable and contingency. We should control the things we can control because there will always be things beyond our control – i.e., others.

Consider the people who have truly touched your life. Chances are they mentored you in some way – i.e., they illuminated and brought out a passion that you developed into a strength. The teacher/mentor/coach truly demonstrated leadership by communicating to you in a clear, respectful, stimulating, and consistent manner. He or she inspired you to reach higher.

Effective coaches ask questions that lead you to take a step back and analyze the situation from a different perspective. Asking questions is a powerful leadership tool, and the hardest ones to answer are those you ask yourself: What happened? Why? What could I have done differently? Why didn't this occur at the time? How can I ensure a better outcome the next time?

Coaching requires different skills and approaches based on where an individual is with regard to performance. If you're new to a team or have a new member on your team, the first order of business is to establish trust and set performance standards so you can assess performance and results. Your team will be assessing whether they can trust you, whether you care about them, and if you are committed to their success. The best way to answer those concerns is to do what's right, do your best, and treat others the way you would like to be treated (*simple stuff you learn at an early age, but behavior that requires constant tweaks and reminders*). When it comes to assessing performance, the coach provides feedback to reinforce the required behaviors.

In "Coaching for Improved Work Performance" by Ferdinand F. Fournies, the author outlines a straightforward, five-step process for most coaching opportunities, and these can be adapted to coaching in a variety of environments. The five steps are especially helpful when feedback requires managing poor performance or disruptive and negative people:

1. Get agreement from the person you're coaching that a problem exists. This is the hardest and most time-consuming part because you are asking someone who may not have high self-awareness to focus on how his or her behavior affects others and how those behaviors take away from the team's ability to deliver necessary results. Getting agreement that a problem exists is also important because if you can't get agreement, there is no sense going forward with other steps because you will not end up with a personalized commitment to change behavior.

2. Once you have agreement on the problem area, mutually discuss alternative solutions. You will get the best results if the person being coached has a lot of say-so in the solution – the "how" he or she will improve. This is also where you will see commitment to change.

3. Mutually agree on the action to be taken to solve the problem, and be clear that you both have the same expectations for what will occur – i.e., what will change, when, and how will that change be measured.

4. Follow-up to measure results. You can't expect what you don't inspect. To measure is to manage.

5. Recognize any achievement when it occurs, and most importantly, catch people doing things right!

Take Away

As mentioned in the Introduction, coaches who have had a positive influence on your life taught you something – or rather, helped you see something you otherwise wouldn't: something about yourself. Coaches are people who have the ability hold a special mirror in front of you that provides insight that others cannot. This comes from understanding a person's values and beliefs and elevating that person's own esteem and expectations.

Ensure you have defined your own core set of unwavering values (e.g., optimistic attitude, humility, courage, ethical behavior, honesty, dependability, etc.). Create an environment with trusted friends by not being defensive, and those friends will be open to providing constructive feedback without reservation.

Make sure you remove the blind spots and confront weaknesses that can prevent you from reaching your full potential. Have an action plan to leverage strengths, minimize weaknesses, and exploit opportunities to reach your goals.

Self-Reliant Leadership is synonymous with knowing which questions to ask yourself and having the courage to answer them and act.

How do you evaluate yourself?

How do you evaluate others?

Do you have the humility to provide the following responses to the people you lead?

> *"I don't know."*
> *"I was wrong."*
> *"I'm sorry."*
> *"I don't understand."*
> *"Would you help me?"*
> *"What do you think?"*
> *"What would you do?"*

Unless commitment is made, there are only promises and hopes; but no plans.

–Peter Drucker, writer, management
consultant

Chapter 4 – Adaptability and Discipline

Adaptability is not imitation. It means power of
resistance and assimilation.
> –Mahatma Gandhi, political and
> ideological leader

Perpetual motion. It has defined my whole life. When I was a kid, my parents would ask me how fast I could run around the outside of the house so they could time me. I was always trying to beat my personal best. What I didn't realize at the time was they were getting me to expend energy to settle down before supper. In the 1970s, the simple term to describe kids like me was "hyperactive."[1] My parents didn't know how to channel my excess energy, so they merely drained it. Later, as a lifelong runner, I learned that even a little extra speed comes at an exponentially high energy cost. A small hill at a jog is no big deal, but that same little hill during a race could feel like Mount Everest. I learned that what separates the runners of equal ability on those hills is their disciplined ability to adapt and endure suffering a little more than the other racers. In other words, understanding when and how to channel

---

1 See Thom Hartmann's book "ADD: A Different Perception" for his Hunter and Farmer Approach to ADD/ADHD.

energy for that extra edge is a critical determinant of success – especially for leaders.

I was barely 17 years old and just a few months into my senior year when I joined the Army in a delayed-entry program on January 29, 1979. There were three times early on when I wondered if I was self-disciplined enough for the Army and if I could adapt to a completely new life.

The first came while still in high school. A new movie came out with Robert De Niro called "The Deer Hunter." De Niro portray a Green Beret soldier, and I was anxious to see how this elite unit would be portrayed, considering the last movie I saw on Special Forces was the famous one with John Wayne – "The Green Berets." Well, the movie was violent and focused on Vietnam prisoners of war and their inadequacy to adapt to civilian life when the war was over. The movie made me seriously question my choice, and I started to realize that not only was I about to lose my innocence, but I could be in for some serious physical hardships. In my large high school class, there was only one other student who was planning to enter the military, and I consoled myself knowing that my impending service was a noble calling. I also believed I was tough enough to handle any adversity, and my assumption about capabilities would certainly be challenged in the not too distant future.

The second doubt I had about my service came during my second day in the Army. I was in my bunk, on top of my sheets, with a newly shaved head prickling my scalp against the stiff pillowcase, lying in the rigid position of attention. Why? Because the drill sergeant told us to fall asleep at attention! In the distance, I could hear people celebrating the Fourth of July and wondered to myself, "Why am I here?" This was completely voluntary, and I did this – to myself!

The final time I questioned my decision came a few weeks later while still in basic training. One moment I was shining my boots, talking with my buddy, and the next moment the brim of the drill sergeant's hat was pressed against the bridge of my nose while I stood rigid in utter terror. Drill Sergeant Hauser was screaming at me because he heard me say, "The 40-foot rappelling exercise we just completed was a piece of cake – not scary at all!" For some reason, this cockiness was a "major" infraction, and I was doing all I could to keep my eyes open while being screamed at and sprayed with saliva. My drill sergeant always reminded me of the cartoon version of the Tasmanian Devil, and with his eyes going wild, he forever stamped that image into my head. As he continued to scream and ask questions I couldn't process, my mind wandered. I wondered how I ended up in this place and whether my decision to join the Army would be a "good" decision for my future. It sure didn't seem like a good decision at that moment.

I learned a lot about myself in basic training through my interaction with other trainees and the drill sergeants. Many of the people who signed up for the Army in the late 1970s had limited options, and some were even given the choice of jail or the Army by a judge. Some of the soldiers were coming from far rougher environments than anything the Army could throw at us, and it was an eye-opener for me to be around some pretty tough people. Because I was coming from the Miami area, many of the soldiers in my basic training platoon called me Miami, and I adapted to yet another nickname.

During the first part of basic training, the drill sergeant assigned squad leaders based on their physical characteristics. I was obviously not picked; however, my squad leader got caught leaving the area and lost his leadership position after just a few weeks. The drill sergeant had noticed that I assumed a role in coaching other soldiers and picked me to be the new squad leader. I was more organized and had picked up on things quicker than some of the other soldiers. For example, memorizing rank, parts of the rifle, military drill, etc. So here I was, the smallest soldier in the platoon. I was in charge of a kid who just got demoted and an assortment of characters who weren't accustomed to taking orders in any form – from anyone. I adapted and chose to coach and collaborate rather than dictate. My efforts paid off, as I was picked by the drill sergeants as the top trainee of the platoon. I competed for trainee of the cycle for the company by writing a speech and going to an interview. I kept the speech I wrote – a 17-year-old's perspective after six weeks in the Army – and listed below are a few excerpts regarding my adaptation:

Reflecting back to day one of the cycle, I remember getting off the cattle car with sixty wide-eyed, scared people, then seeing a man in a "Smokey the Bear hat" who we learned to call Drill Sergeant, or "Knock 'em out!" Up until this moment, most of us had a pretty relaxed life either going to school or working a measly eight hours a day, five days a week.

A lot of changes occurred in our lives these past six weeks, both mentally and physically. We went from a mob of people to a highly disciplined group of people. Our attitudes became positive, and we learned to perform in a military manner.

I didn't win the top spot for the company, but I gained the much-needed confidence I would need for the difficult training that awaited me.

After basic training, I attended the basic medic course at Fort Sam Houston, Texas, followed by Airborne School at Fort Benning, Georgia. In the 1970s, the Army had a bad reputation for not honoring the enlistment contracts, and I was nervous the whole time that I really wasn't signed up for Special Forces. Over the years, Special Forces has changed the policy that allows men right off the street to sign up. In hindsight, I personally think it makes more sense to have soldiers with "conventional" experience try out for the elite unit because one of the main missions of Special Forces is to teach and train indigenous soldiers in conventional tactics. After successfully completing Airborne School, my fear was alleviated, as I was shipped north to Fort Bragg, North Carolina, to attend the Special Forces Qualification Course pre-phase training. An "A" team from the 7th Special Forces Group prepped us for phase one through training on map reading and patrolling. The full-time tactical NCOs pushed us physically with an assortment of tests, runs, and rucksack marches. They didn't harass us, but they certainly didn't pamper us either.

Live as brave men; and if fortune is adverse, front its blows with brave hearts.
—Cicero, Roman philosopher,
statesman, lawyer, political theorist

While snowed in, awaiting transportation from Camp Mackall back to Fort Bragg (about 50 miles), I wrote a letter to my family at the completion of the first phase of the Special Forces Qualification Course. I'm not sure why I never mailed it, but I probably thought the letter was too personal and showed too much vulnerability. Reading it after all these years, it's good to see what I was thinking without the worry of a distorted memory. I inserted footnotes to provide an explanation or a frame of reference, and the letter in its entirety follows *without* corrections:

Dearest Family,

Well, I left Fort Bragg on an 80-pac (cattle car) with my newly issued mother-father-girlfriend-brother-sister and best friend, my M-16.[2] When we got to Camp Mackall, we were herded into our tar-papered shacks and ordered to dump our belongings onto our plywood slab, or bunk. The mean "Green Beanies" then stormed in and proceeded to confiscate and search for contraband.[3] They even took my long underwear shirt you bought me. They said, "You're

---

2 M-16 was the standard rifle that was issued to soldiers.
3 The contraband they were looking for was primarily food and vitamins. They didn't want anyone to have an unfair advantage.

not planning on being cold while you're here, are you?"[4]

The next day we ran to the airfield, and chuted up, and sat and waited for the plane in five-degree weather. That was the coldest day in my life. It was a very windy day, and they dropped us one-half mile west of the drop zone. We jumped a C-130 aircraft, and I was third man out, second stick.[5] I had about five feet of tangles in my suspension lines and almost had to pop my reserve because I was descending so fast. We jumped at an altitude of only 1,500 feet because of the wind. I almost landed on the smoke[6] and two trucks because I couldn't control my chute. When we exited the aircraft, we literally ran out after each other. It was kind of scary.

The next day we started map reading. It also snowed eight inches in one afternoon. We also had a snowball fight with the other platoon. That was the <u>one</u> fun thing I did at Camp Mackall. We also started running and rucksack marches that week at 0500 hours every morning. Talk about getting your butt kicked! I also got tendinitis on my right Achilles tendon in my heel. It's getting better, though there's nothing they can do for it. One day we went rucking in three inches of ice on the roads. A lot of people got hurt bad. I came in 5 minutes after the main body of the formation so I had to do it again that night. That was the first and last ruck I fell out of.[7]

---

4 There were three record-low temperatures at Fort Bragg in February 1980 that still stand to this day.

5 "Stick" refers to a group of parachutists jumping at one- or two-second intervals from the same exit door of an aircraft on the same drop zone.

6 "Smoke" refers to smoke grenades that are popped during airborne operations so the jumpers can see the direction of the wind.

7 Running was always easy, but the rucksack marches made my shins feel like someone lit a blowtorch to them. It was probably because I had to uncomfortably stretch my short stride, because if you got caught jogging, the instructors would make you do push-ups with your rucksack on. The rucksacks usually weighed 35 to 45 pounds for "exercise," plus other gear.

Then we went out in the field for three days to do land navigation. It's really fun sleeping in the snow (ha-ha). The stakes we had to find were white and two to three miles apart. Plus you were by yourself in the day and night part which didn't help. Oh yeah, you had to pass a map test and you had to find so many stakes[8] in four hours in the day, and four hours at night.

Then we started general subjects. Survival, field expedient direction finding, killing and skinning animals, and how to teach. We had to plan and give a class. Then we went to the field for three days to learn survival. I ate two tablespoons of rice a day for 3 days. I never knew hunger until then. I am now thankful every time I eat. Here's a list of what I thought of sitting around starving one night:

Pizza	Fondue	Tacos	M&M's
Hamburgers	French Onion Soup	Chip Ahoy's	Marshmallow cream
French Fries	Sub Sandwiches	Oreos	Crunchy Peanut butter
Onion Rings	BLT's	Hostess Cupcakes	White Bread
Ice Cream	Steak	Chocolate cream-filled donuts	Garlic Bread
Pretzels	Nacho Cheese Doritos	Cinnamon rolls	
Cider	Snickers bars	Chocolate pudding	
Malted Milk Balls	Nestle Crunch bars	Cap'n Crunch	
Popcorn	Kentucky Fried Chicken	Red licorice	
Tuna, Noodles & Peas	Breakfast sausage	Chocolate & white milk	
Apple Pie			

Then we rappelled chopper and cliff style.[9] It was a blast! Then we rucked back (still hungry). Then we ran a mile. Then we ran a mile and half, 28-obstacle course. At the end, I had to low crawl 200 yards because I didn't make it up the last 50-foot

8 The stakes were metal poles about four feet high and painted white so you could see them in the woods – except we were doing the navigation in the snow!
9 "Cliff style" meant coming down a wooden tower, whereas "chopper" meant rappelling off a chopper skid with no wall to brace yourself.

rope. I then learned what total harassment and pain was.[10] Then we got our first meal in three and half days, which I proceeded to throw up. By the way, I weighed 105 when I got back from survival. I think I weigh about 120 now – I'm not sure. I am a lot skinnier though. Then came patrolling which we had to pass the hardest test I've taken since I've been in the army. Then we went to the field for one week with an 80-pound rucksack.[11] We ate pretty good out there, but I only got eight hours of sleep that week.[12] Then we came back. Oh, on the one-week FTX[13], we each had to be the Patrol Leader and we had to show knowledge of patrolling and leadership qualities. I was told by the instructor I should not be a private because I am definitely a leader and not a follower.[14] I then remembered dad telling me that himself. A small note – we had seven minutes to eat our meals

---

10 I left out that this was a real crucible for me. I was one of about ten soldiers who failed the last obstacle – a rope climb. The instructor made us low-crawl back through other obstacles and kicked dirt on us and pleaded for us to quit. He even said he would buy us a steak if we quit. It just made me mad and determined, but I did have a moment or two where I truly questioned my resolve.

11 The rucksack weight represented upward of 76 percent of my body weight. Though I wished the weight we carried was proportional, I knew that wasn't fair to the other soldiers, but I often wondered how I would have fared on marches if we had all carried the same proportion of weight.

12 Another thing I failed to mention was that I hallucinated a lot with the sleep deprivation. Because the instructors were Vietnam vets, the training focused on their experiences, and I often saw Vietnamese soldiers coming at me in black pajamas and Asian conical hats. At one point, I actually fell asleep while walking and face-planted myself in the snow.

13 Field Training Exercise

14 Being identified as having leadership potential on this exercise was a defining moment – more than what I initially wrote. I had been picked to lead towards the end of the exercise when everyone was dead tired. Half of the soldiers I was in charge of were senior to me, and the instructor told me I had done better than some of the NCOs in the patrol.

every day.[15] In other words, they fed us just enough to keep us alive.[16] I don't even remember what girls look like, or food tastes like, or heat feels like. I also got minor frostbite on my fingers and toes.[17] I came down with tendonitis, bronchitis, and a severe case of conjunctivitis (which is pink eye). I was told not to mention I had bronchitis because they could kick me out of SF if they found out.[18] I managed eight cold showers in the month of February so it wasn't too bad. Right now, I'm just waiting to go back to Bragg. There was twelve inches of snow on the ground yesterday and we were playing G.I. Joe in it. Bummer – we'll probably leave tomorrow. Helicopters tried to come out here, but if they land in the snow, it will wreck something on the aircraft. So I guess I'll just sit in this classroom with the other 49 guys. Only two-thirds of the class made it. Actually, that's very good. Also, the song about the Green Beret's is very true – every word.[19]

I know this sounds like a lot of sniveling and crying, but I think someone should appreciate my thirty days of blood, sweat and tears. I wonder what it will feel like to sleep in linen without a weapon?

-Love, Your one and only Sonny

---

15 This included the time we had to open our C-ration cans with a tiny opener called a P-38. We got pretty good at opening cans fast!

16 It would be interesting to know how many calories we were burning with exercise and shivering to stay warm versus the calories we consumed. I'm sure there was a deficit, but I'm not so sure we were near starving!

17 The frostbite was actually on my nose and ears as well and has bothered me ever since, so I'm not sure how minor it was. Our clothes back then were woefully inadequate. We used some wool but mostly cotton.

18 I had one more bout of bronchitis when I was a lieutenant in Panama, which is described later in the book.

19 Based on the documentaries I have seen of today's Special Forces Qualification Course, I think today's soldiers are as tough as ever. They certainly know much more about nutrition and fitness than we did.

I think completing that particular phase of training provided a greater sense of accomplishment than earning my green beret at the conclusion of the all the training because I was most worried about passing this phase. I knew the medical portion would be tough, but I knew it was primarily academic, which I wasn't worried about. This particular phase had me spooked because of the high attrition rate. Moreover, this phase really tested my will. I knew I wouldn't quit, but there were plenty of times I questioned my resolve, and there was a time or two when I envied the guys who got hurt and *got* to be evacuated because I knew they'd soon be warm and surrounded by nurses!

Much to my chagrin, my integrity came into question on one specific day. The instructors always supported teamwork on the rucksack marches, and there was one particularly big guy who was always there for me, encouraging me, because he knew I struggled under the same weight everyone else carried. His name was Lowen and he was from Seattle. There was even a time when he had his rifle across his chest and parallel to the ground, and he encouraged me to hold on while he just pushed through. Prior to meals, we had to either climb a rope, do pull-ups, or do chin-ups. I was behind Lowen, waiting for him to do the requisite number of chin-ups so he could grab his chow, and he was struggling. I started yelling the same encouragement to him that he provided to me during rucksack marches. If he could pull me along, the least I could do was get under him and help him execute his chin-ups.

I was wrong. I wasn't hiding anything, but an instructor called me out for cheating. Cheating? I was being a team player! Lowen and I were called into the headquarters shack where we stood at attention and got chewed out. The instructors said they were going to terminate the both of us for cheating, but they said I could make a statement before they rendered their final judgment. I went on to tell them about how Lowen had helped me and how I was being a good "buddy" and returning the favor. I don't remember exactly what I said, but I remember being mortified at the prospect of failing, but worse, at having my integrity questioned.

The instructors looked at each other, nodded, and one commenced to speak. He stated that by no means did they condone my actions, but they understood my intentions. With little fanfare, he told us we were still in the course and to get back to our business without haste.

More than anything, this phase taught me the value of adapting to an environment and having the self-discipline to thrive. It also taught me that I would never again put myself in a situation where my integrity would be questioned. It takes a lifetime to build a reputation and a moment to lose one. That was something I wanted no part of. The most valuable lesson was that if you want something bad enough and you're willing to sacrifice comfort and pleasure, the goal is quite attainable.

A great deal has been written about leadership crucibles as severe tests of how people handle adversity, and phase one certainly qualified, from my perspective.[20] How a leader handles adversity and hardship can certainly highlight strengths and weaknesses, and it's good to know how you'll react before leading others because leaders will inevitably be tested with a crisis at some point. In the absence of crisis, leadership can be collaborative, managerial, and mundane. It can also involve strategy development, planning, and contingency preparations. In a crisis, a leader's decisiveness and ability to focus will be tested, and it's good to know how you'll respond when others are dependent on your ability to pass the ultimate test.

Take Away

Reading this book is a start toward *your* education as a leader. As you progress in your career, it will be important

---

20 For a thorough review of this principle, see the Harvard Business Review article "Crucibles of Leadership" by Warren G. Bennis and Robert J. Thomas, Sept. 1, 2002.

for you to figure out how to be your own teacher – an active learner.

What's the best way to honestly capture your thoughts, ideas, experiences, feelings, frustrations, plans, and adaptations to those plans? A journal. Do you have the self-discipline to *openly* and *honestly* capture your thoughts, ideas, experiences, feelings, frustrations, plans, and adaptations to those plans so you can continuously improve? How else can you reflect back and learn from those mistakes you know you'll make? How else can you develop a navigational chart for yourself and the people you will develop as future leaders? A journal can be the control mechanism for all you do. It becomes the ultimate self-evaluation, above and beyond any feedback you will ever receive – if you're honest with yourself.

Self-Reliant Leadership is synonymous with knowing which questions to ask yourself and having the courage to answer them and act.

How can self-awareness ensure you'll do the right thing in the face of adversity?

How does your life story fit with your passion, purpose, values, and vision?

What would you do with your life if you knew you couldn't fail?

I believe that the rendering of useful service is the common duty of mankind and that only in the purifying fire of sacrifice is the dross of selfishness consumed and the greatness of the human soul set free.

–John D. Rockefeller, German-
American oil magnate
and philanthropist

Chapter 5 – As an Art ... from the Heart

"People become motivated when you guide them to the source of their own power."
        –Anita Roddick, British
        businesswoman and human
        rights activist

O f the people you have personally encountered in your life so far, think about the person who has had the most profound impact on you. Even if you didn't conjure up a teacher, chances are the person you thought of is someone who taught you something. And chances are what he or she taught you wasn't a particular subject per se, but something that person illuminated within you. That person brought out a passion in you that others may not have seen. You could say that person, that coach, demonstrated leadership. That person guided you to create a vision for yourself while being respectful, stimulating, and inspiring.

My Special Forces training as a medic consisted of a number of phases. Each phase required successful completion to move on to the next phase. Unlike pre-phase and phase one, phase two actually consisted of three phases: medical training at Fort Sam Houston in San Antonio, Texas; hospital on-the-job training at Fort Sill in Lawton, Oklahoma; and "med lab" back at Fort Bragg, North Carolina. The first two phases culminated in phase three, where the soldiers who had gone through specialized medic, communications, demolitions, and weapons training came together in an exercise that simulated the work of an "A" team mission. For medics, all three phases lasted a full year, and I was with many of the same people for the entire year. Our attrition rate was highest during the medical phase of the training due to the academic rigor for which many were unprepared. What I remember most about the year of training isn't what I learned about medicine, soldiering, or special operations, but what I learned about people – and myself.

During the year of training, I went from barely 18 to barely 19 years old, and most of my peers were in their early 20s; some were even older. I was not only the smallest person, but one of the youngest as well. I was immature, and though I knew the woods, I was far from street-smart. The extended training provided a great opportunity to learn from peers because we were together nearly twenty-four hours a day for a full year during physical, mental, and emotional testing.

I learned the advice my neighbor/mentor, George Callahan, provided was completely valid. I did need to work with everyone. More importantly, I needed to choose my close friends very carefully. I was learning what "carefully" meant to me because my core values were still being forged. A lot of the soldiers who signed up for Special Forces had similar backgrounds. They came from broken homes; they were trying to prove something to an uncle, father, or brother; and they generally came from the South or tough areas of New England. Most had already faced a fair amount of adversity, and I don't remember anyone who had come from a privileged background. What made us different was how we handled adversity and the very personal motivations that kept us going during highly stressful situations. It wasn't a course you could complete if you didn't truly want it. There were plenty of times I asked myself what I was doing there and reminded myself that I had ultimately volunteered for the hardship and suffering; I knew that adversity was worth the outcome I envisioned.

There were three fellow students I learned a great deal from during the training, and all for very different reasons. The first was a former bouncer from Texas who had already completed some community college. He was big, strong, smart, and quiet – sullen in a way. For the first phase of the training, we lived in old World War II barracks, and they had been abused over the years. My fellow students offered no mercy to those barracks and collected martial arts contraband at weekend forays to pawnshops. At any given time, there were Chinese throwing stars being hurled from one end of the open-bay barracks to the other, terminating firmly in metal wall lockers. There were also nunchucks, switchblades, and other "self-defense" implements. In the barracks at night, the ex-bouncer took it upon himself to teach me how to fight. He thought I needed toughening and that I should know how to street fight because with my size I would never be in a "fair" fight. I agreed that if I ever did fight, the other guy wouldn't be my size! At first he'd spar with me with one hand behind his back, but after popping his jaw for the first time, he always used both hands. The training would usually end with me calling for mercy. The ex-bouncer would eventually get the same first-duty assignment as me, and he really had a good heart. My initial impression of him being sullen was actually the façade of a very intellectual person who cared deeply about people. He instinctively knew that to serve others meant continuous self-improvement, and he was always open to new ideas, experiences, and people. His mentoring boosted my self-confidence and helped me become more aware of others who could benefit from coaching and mentoring.

The second person who had a significant impact on me was a sergeant who was old enough to have a wife and two kids. In fact, his age had a little to do with the fact that he was one of the weakest students involved in the training. Despite his physical limitations, he was a keen observer of group dynamics. As the senior member of our class, he was designated the class leader and did a great job of balancing the needs of different cliques that inevitably appeared within our small training class.

Fort Sam Houston is primarily a medical training post, and in contrast to those of us going through Special Forces training, most of the soldiers on post weren't particularly oriented to being hard-core soldiers. That's a nice way of saying we thought we were "special" compared to the other soldiers. This was a sentiment that was shared within our group, but on a shameful night, one of the small cliques decided to do something quite drastic. Fed up with the loud music coming from a nearby barracks, the clique decided to start a fight in the middle of the night. None of the soldiers in my class were hurt, but a lot of people who were targeted were hurt badly. I didn't know of anything until the MPs woke us and rousted us from our bunks to stand in a line outside in our underwear. On a chilly night, we were lined up so the victims could walk the line and identify the assailants. At one point, an MP found a two-foot broom handle by my locker that I twirled like a drumstick while trying to stay awake on fireguard duty. The MP knew the stick was next to a wall locker labeled "Rutherford," and he barked my name and ordered me to take one step forward. When I did, I heard snickering from the MPs and my classmates, which I knew was because of my size. They must have thought I couldn't have hurt anyone, because after the laughing stopped, they told me to step back in line without asking me a single question.

The incident was worse than first imagined because most of the soldiers in our class were white, and most of the soldiers who were beaten were black. As a punishment to the entire class, the generals on post decided to move our class to an old remote barracks without hot water. The location was far from any other unit. Our class leader's skills were tested in profound ways as he balanced keeping the class focused on graduating and mending unit and race relations across the post.

Long before I learned what Situational Leadership was, I saw this NCO demonstrate different leadership styles for different people in different circumstances. Despite multiple distractions, I was afforded plenty of attention and received a promotion to private first class during the whole ordeal. It taught me that a leader can't let attention be consumed by disciplinary problems and that your best return is when you grow and develop high-potential people. As an art, from the heart.

The third person I learned a great deal from was someone I didn't like or respect. Most of us tended to be on the skinny side, and this guy was muscular, acne-scarred, and had a superiority complex because he had a master's degree. He told everyone he just signed up for Special Forces to acquire the military experience that would make him a viable candidate for the CIA. I sensed contempt for me because I didn't conform to his image of who "should" be in Special Forces. If it were up to him, qualifications would include a body type. This wise guy from the Northeast taught me an invaluable lesson. Everyone has some insecurity, but a lot of the bad behavior I have seen stems from people who have a lot of insecurities. These insecurities manifest themselves in bullying, turf wars, a general lack of self-awareness, and the affect the behavior has on other people.

When this wise guy realized that I was indeed going to pass the course and earn my beret, he started telling me that people who saw me would see someone who didn't fit the image of a Special Forces soldier. He was projecting his own thoughts and conveyed that I would make an easy target for people to test how tough Special Forces really was. His main focus was that someone would try to steal or knock my beret off my head. Honestly, it never occurred to me that someone might want to prove how tough he was by starting a fight with a Green Beret. I realized one thing from this bully's behavior. As I kept quiet, I ultimately had power over him. In the end, he couldn't control my reaction, and if I ignored him, it diminished his efforts to influence me and others around me. In the entire time I wore a beret, not a single person ever tried to start a fight or steal my cover. The bully's paranoia was really a reflection of his own insecurity, and it was only contagious if I let it be.

When I was going through the final phases of my Special Forces training, the more insightful and proactive students went looking for jobs. It might sound peculiar to hear that a soldier needs to interview for a job, but in Special Forces, not all "A" teams are equal. In fact, prior to a mission, it's typical for three or four teams to compete with each other to win the privilege of being assigned a mission. The teams would present a compelling case to a panel of senior officers and NCOs as to why they were best prepared to successfully complete the mission's objectives. Enriched by this culture, each team would take on the personality of its leader to a greater degree than typical. At 19 years old, I can't claim I was one of the insightful and proactive students, but in hindsight, I was lucky nonetheless. For some reason, I stood out as a potential instructor for the Special Forces School itself and was asked to consider a role teaching and running the camp's aid station that was 50 miles from the nearest physician or hospital.

I accepted without much consideration, as I was flattered to be singled out. The job was to teach Special Forces candidates basic medical skills and a survival class we called "The Kill Class." It was a class where we showed starving students during survival training how to kill, butcher, and prepare animals to eat (i.e., goats, rabbits, and chickens). In addition, we provided medical aid for the students since the compound was so isolated from the main fort. This meant a great deal of medical autonomy and daily experiences with injuries like wounds, broken bones, and infectious illnesses. The students lived in tarpaper shacks stacked like cords of wood with no heat, and they received little sleep and meager meals.

The teaching assignment involved learning how to create and deliver effective instruction. In 1980, we even had access to a new technology whereby we could record ourselves delivering instruction and play it back on something called a videotape. More importantly, I learned I really enjoyed teaching. I saw it as a performance wherein one could educate, inspire, and motivate. I liked the research, the preparation, the rehearsal, the performance, and most of all, I enjoyed getting positive feedback from the students. Now, many years later, I can reflect back on a career that has contained some sort of teaching component in every assignment. It's interesting that a certain sergeant named O'Connell saw that aptitude and passion in me before he even knew me. I have derived the most personal satisfaction from teaching, training, and coaching because they provide an opportunity where leadership development can be facilitated.

Take Away

The goal of leadership is to gain willing followers who are committed and not merely compliant. Leadership is ultimately a balancing act, much like the concepts of yin and yang – two opposing but complementary and interdependent forces found in all things. Leadership, like yin and yang, is something that requires balance – as one increases, the other tends to decrease and vice versa. A highly energetic person can also be a very impatient person; that is, a strength can ultimately be a weakness.

Self-reliance can serve as a fulcrum on which to balance compassion and discipline as indicators of leadership effectiveness. Articulating where you're going, how you'll get there, and why it's important is the mechanical part of leadership. The *art* is in working towards a balance to build trust and gain a voluntary commitment from those you seek to influence (also known as emotional intelligence).

For example, missions need to be accomplished, but can only be done through the successful management/balancing of human relationships. A leader needs strength of character, but also needs a measure of humility. A leader needs to do the right things while also managing to do things right. Tasks need to be accomplished, processes need to be initiated and followed, and creativity needs a good dose of pragmatic behavior. One can drive compliance, but having true commitment is another matter. Micromanagement is the bane of most teams, while unchecked autonomy is not conducive to great team accomplishments either.

In the end, it's really about communicating a vision in such a way that the leader is able to gain willing, engaged, and motivated followers who are truly committed, not blindly obedient drones. The vision needs to strike a balance between expending energy on short-term objectives while achieving long-term goals so people are engaged, energized, and passionate.

As in the examples listed above, one force unchecked can compromise the opposing force and vice versa. The key is to keep your values aligned with expectations and have a positive attitude that you can coach yourself to identify areas where your leadership requires more *balance*.

Self-Reliant Leadership is synonymous with knowing which questions to ask yourself and having the courage to answer them and act.

How do you guide people to the source of their own power?

What can you do to increase your awareness of the things that motivate others (i.e., empathy and emotional intelligence)?

What, in particular, makes people rise to tough challenges?

You may not currently have a gifted and caring mentor, but consider contacting and interviewing a local business or community leader and his/her team to learn firsthand different leadership and coaching principles. Ask the leader about performance-management issues (e.g., hiring, firing, and promoting) and organization-development issues (e.g., culture and structure). Is there alignment between what the leader says and what the team does?

In every difficult situation is potential value. Believe this, then begin looking for it.

–Norman Vincent Peale, author of
"The Power of Positive Thinking"

Chapter 6 – Learned Optimism

"Of the tens of millions of American men below five foot six, a grand total of ten in my sample have reached the level of CEO, which says that being short is probably as much a handicap to corporate success as being a woman or an African American."

–Malcolm Gladwell, best-selling author

I believe we only possess two innate *controllables*. That is, *where* you spend your time and *how* you respond to your environment. How you respond to your environment is analogous to choosing your attitude by way of controlling your emotional response to other people and situations. At my first assignment after receiving my beret, I had the extreme good fortune of observing firsthand three remarkable leaders whose stories were literally the stuff of legends. If it weren't for their optimism in the face of calamitous conditions, they wouldn't have survived, successfully led their men, nor inspired others to this day.

The keynote speaker at my Special Forces graduation ceremony was a major who had just come back on active duty after a six-year hiatus. While I served at the John F. Kennedy Special Warfare Center and School, the Army's special operations university, I had the honor of working with a man who had a phenomenal story of demonstrating hope and optimism in dire circumstances. His name was James Nicholas (Nick) Rowe, and he was from McAllen, Texas. He graduated from the United States Military Academy at West Point in 1960 and became a member of the Special Forces stationed as an advisor in the Mekong Delta. In 1963, he and two other soldiers were captured by the Vietcong, and he was taken and kept prisoner in the U Minh Forest, known as the "Forest of Darkness," in southern Vietnam. He was held for five years, spending most of the time bound and suffering from dysentery, in a small bamboo cage. He was hopeful for escape, yet realistic with how long he might be held against his will. He confronted the brutal facts of his situation and did everything possible to survive physically, mentally, and emotionally. He controlled how he responded to his environment and prevented his captors from entering his remaining area of control and stealing his hope.

In 1968, on his way to be executed, he managed to escape and was rescued eleven days later by a U.S. helicopter. The crew on the helicopter came close to shooting him, as he was wearing black pajamas – the same "uniform" the Vietcong wore. The crew chief on the helicopter noticed he had a full beard, and therefore, couldn't have been Vietnamese. He was one of only thirty-four American prisoners of war to escape in Vietnam and the only one to have escaped from the Vietcong.

Rowe subsequently wrote a book called "Five Years to Freedom" in which he described his imprisonment, torture, and solitude. What sustained Rowe the most was the Duty, Honor, Country motto he learned at West Point, which General MacArthur made famous. Rowe had the unwavering optimism that the enemy could not break his spirit and that he would eventually be rescued or escape.

The seminal work on the topic of logotherapy was done by Viktor Frankl, who wrote "Man's Search for Meaning."

Frankl, a Holocaust survivor, learned through the horrors of losing his freedom and his family that the one thing the Nazis could not take away from him was how he responded to the environment – which became his focus. Logotherapy purports that the most powerful motivating and driving force in humans is to find meaning in one's life.

I found Colonel Rowe to be a fascinating man. Some of the men at Camp Mackall had extremely high regard for him while others were quite critical of his vision for the Army's new Survival, Evasion, Resistance, and Escape (SERE) school. I hadn't read Frankl's book before my acquaintance with Colonel Rowe. Considering Rowe was extremely well read, I am certain he must have read that book at some point. In retrospect, I would like to have asked him if that knowledge had helped sustain him. He knew authors, politicians, and was focused on a singular, genuine mission: He wanted to thoroughly prepare soldiers for the ultimate sacrifice in times of war and to learn how to be optimistic when hope was all but lost.

When I was deciding whether to reenlist or depart active duty for college, ROTC, and the reserves, Colonel Rowe asked me to be the medic at his new SERE school. He said I would work closely with a psychologist he was going to hire. Though he was extremely charismatic and convincing, my desire to advance my education was stronger. Plus, I honestly believed that being associated with the SERE school would, over time, be psychologically taxing.

On the 25th of September 1987 – some five years later – I would see Colonel Rowe again. He was a lieutenant colonel at the time but was promotable to colonel. He was giving a lecture to the military intelligence interrogation platoon at Fort Ord, California. I had the opportunity to introduce him to my wife the next day at a parade ceremony. Ever the politician, his gaze would fix upon the person he was speaking to, and it was easy to see how his charm had served him well when selling his visionary ideas. The SERE school still serves its purpose today, but sadly, nineteen months after I saw Colonel Rowe in April 1989, he was assassinated in the Philippines by a communist rebel. He always typified *learned optimism* based on a code that spoke to him. Inscribed on his tombstone in Arlington National Cemetery is a poem he wrote in 1964, while a POW, that typified his sanguinity:

> *So look up ahead at times to come,*
> *despair is not for us.*
> *We have a world and more to see,*
> *while this remains behind.*

One of the signatures on my Special Forces Qualification Course certificate is that of Ola Mize, Director, Special Forces School. The first time I remember meeting Colonel Mize was when he came into the aid station asking for a specific brand of hand lotion. At the time, it struck me as an odd request from a soldier, especially since someone had told me he was a Medal of Honor recipient and had killed thirteen enemy soldiers in the Korean War with an E-tool![1] He was 49 years old when I met him but not a whole lot bigger than me. Some people wore a beret better than others, and his beret just looked like it belonged on his head. He always had a squint to his eyes, and in a gruff, pirate-like voice would say, "Argh, whatcha doin', peanut?" Again, another nickname, but I didn't mind the attention from the colonel. He retired to his home state of Alabama shortly after I met him, but it was great to see his way with the troops. He had been an enlisted man before he was an officer, and that earned him a lot of respect, along with the Medal of Honor award. By my count, his Medal of Honor citation states he killed eleven soldiers, and there was no mention of how he killed them, but he did direct an artillery unit to fire dangerously close to his position. I learned later

---

1 E-tool is short for entrenching tool, which is a short, collapsible shovel/spade.

that he was initially rejected by the Army for being too light at 120 pounds but pestered the recruiters to allow him to join. It was with Colonel Mize I started to realize that people who face adversity and prejudice can have a strengthened resolve with no equal. I often wondered if Colonel Mize's bravery was in part from his determination to show that a person's character cannot be judged by appearance alone.

We got word that a new officer was coming in as the officer in charge (OIC) of phase-one training and that he was literally tough as nails. His name was Major Robert Howard, and he was the most decorated living soldier in the U.S. military. He was barrel-chested, square-jawed, and scarred. Uncharacteristic of most Special Forces soldiers, he kept his hair more like a Marine than a Special Forces operative. He looked like the soldier I had seen on the brochure for the Green Berets when the recruiter encouraged me to sign up. If his physical appearance wasn't intimidating enough, he had a gaze that made men lower their eyes in submission. He was gruff and tough, and he seemed determined to live up to the hype that surrounded him. Like Colonel Mize, he was an NCO when he was awarded the Medal of Honor. He also called in fire on his own position and retired as a full-bird colonel.

As a platoon sergeant, his unit was attacked by an estimated two-company force. Howard was wounded and his weapon destroyed by a grenade explosion. His Medal of Honor citation read as follows:

"Although unable to walk, and weaponless, 1st Lt. Howard unhesitatingly crawled through a hail of fire to retrieve his wounded leader. Through his outstanding example of indomitable courage and bravery, 1st Lt. Howard was able to rally the platoon into an organized defense force. With complete disregard for his safety, 1st Lt. Howard crawled from position to position, administering first aid to the wounded, giving encouragement to the defenders and directing their fire on the encircling enemy. For 3 1/2 hours, 1st Lt. Howard's small force and supporting aircraft successfully repulsed enemy attacks and finally were in sufficient control to permit the landing of rescue helicopters. 1st Lt. Howard personally supervised the loading of his men and did not leave the bullet-swept landing zone until all were aboard safely."

What I remember most about Colonel Howard is his uncanny ability to know when to push the troops physically and when they needed a pep talk. He had an innate sense for "balance," and his pep talks weren't like those given by a football coach. His talks were about the brotherhood of arms in unbelievably harsh conditions where hope was hard to grasp. He talked about leadership and how the profession of arms was a noble calling, and that combat was the only true crucible for a soldier. He was the only military leader I've witnessed who could bring the troops to tears while inspiring them to new heights. And he believed that physically, mentally, and emotionally challenging training was the only way to prepare leaders for the chaos of combat. It was his way to create leaders who would take care of themselves and their soldiers in extreme conditions.

Even when he was particularly tough on troops, he always believed that with the right attitude, any soldier could overcome any obstacle. Sometimes he would work out with multiple classes of trainees and would literally exhaust himself. More than a few times, I found Howard collapsed on the side of the road during a rucksack march (he was well into his 40s at the time), and I would disobey his order and start an IV on him. He always showed me respect by using my title. "Sergeant Rutherford – I _order_ you to leave me be!" I'd reply, "Sir, we just need to get some fluid in you and you'll be fine – no big deal." From the wounds he suffered in Vietnam, his body was a wreck. He had bad knees, and long-buried shrapnel would surface from inopportune places. He seemed to dehydrate easily – probably because he was pushing so hard to kick the butts of trainees half his age!

Much has been written about Colonel Howard as a highly decorated soldier, and some believe a movie should be made of his life so that a bar can be set for what constitutes a true hero. Colonel Howard's signature is on my first Army Commendation Medal, and that always meant a great deal to me because I knew his standards were uncompromising. I was around Colonel Howard a lot, but I can't say I ever really knew him. I never heard him speak of family, and he seemed to be at the camp all the time. I wondered if he even needed sleep. When he walked in the aid station, it was different from any other officer. I would venture to say that I have never met another person who was more respected. It wasn't for the medals or his physical stamina. Colonel Howard truly believed that we're all capable of much more than we ever thought possible. He knew that special leaders can draw out that optimism so people can be more self-reliant.

Just as I observed when I was a boy, I believe you see peoples' true character when they're wet, cold, tired, and hungry. When people face adversity, you see different things in them than when they're relatively comfortable. *No pain, no change*. It didn't involve combat, but I would remember the examples of Rowe, Mize, and Howard when I experienced my own crucible. My personal test involved being instantaneously uncomfortable after splitting my kneecap into two pieces while mountain biking with friends in a remote area of the Rockies.

It was a Sunday afternoon, and we were on the last, steep mile of a 20-mile loop after a guys' weekend of riding. We started too late and got hit with a severe thunderstorm, which is never good in the mountains. The rain made the trails slick, and I was a few minutes ahead of my friends, descending a steep trail of switchbacks. I hit the side of a large rock with my front tire, and the rock slid in the mud and instantly jerked my wheel and handlebars abruptly to the right at a perpendicular angle to my bike frame. Even though I was only traveling 6.5 miles per hour, my right knee impacted squarely into the end of the handle bar and instantly cracked in half before I hit the ground. Without spilling a drop of blood, the two pieces of my kneecap were contained under the skin. Due to the muscle contractions in my leg, one piece of my kneecap was drifting towards my shin while the other was moving up towards my quadriceps, creating a four-finger gap between the two pieces of what's a small bone to begin with.

As I lay in the mud with my heel under my buttocks, I immediately yelled in pain and for my friends to hear. I yelled twice more, but they were too far back to hear me. I knew exactly what I had done. My first instinct was to straighten my knee because I thought (wrongly) that I might be able to mount my bike and at least make it back to the truck. I was embarrassed, and I didn't want my friends to find me "broken" in the mud. Strangely – feeling embarrassed was my first reaction. After grinding my leg straight and again yelling in pain, I pulled the bike towards me when I quickly realized that I was not going anywhere until my friends arrived. My next thought was, "This is bad, but I am supposed to learn something from this."

The next thing I did was figure out the logistics. I knew that my two friends would have to leave their bikes and walk me down the mountain. I knew the other person, already at the truck, could come back up the trail with one other person to get three bikes while someone drove me to the hospital.

When my friends arrived, they knew the situation was not good – I could see it on their faces. Moreover, they were already exhausted from a weekend of riding, and they knew what laid ahead was going to be grueling. One guy hid the bikes off the trail while the other person found a few sticks to improvise a splint. He used a tire tube and a piece of Velcro to secure the sticks on the sides of my knee after wrapping my knee in a polypropylene shirt. I didn't know it at the time, but the ligaments on both sides of my knee were also torn apart, and the only thing holding my knee together was the two interior ligaments (ACL and MCL) and the skin. This meant that my foot could not be lifted off the ground without excruciating pain. We got down the mountain in a trail that was basically a muddy trough. I was hopping on my left leg and dragging my right leg behind me, toe down. My two friends let me use their forearms as crutches, all while they struggled to walk on the forty-five-degree slopes of the trail.

It took an hour to go down the remaining mile, and at the bottom, there was a shallow stream we needed to cross. There was a footbridge, and I told my friends that there was no way I was going to dangle my leg on a six-inch bridge. We were going straight through the cold water! After thirty minutes on a rough dirt road and thirty minutes on a paved road, we arrived at the hospital. It was a slow day, as paramedics, nurses, and the ER doctor all helped "extract" me from the front passenger seat of my truck. It took another hour for the X-rays and other tests before I got some pain medication. The medical personnel didn't account for my 128 pounds and loaded me up pretty good. That's when my friends enjoyed exacerbating the paranoia that had set in by constantly moving my keys, phone, and wallet around the room.

Three-and-a-half hours later, we arrived at the hospital in Denver where the orthopedic surgeon stated that he was too tired to do the surgery, and one of his partners was a better knee guy. He said that it would be best to wait until the next day, and with that, I was sent home with a broken knee, a worried wife who had met me at the hospital, and in an opiate fog that would last another six days.

I had innovative surgery the next day performed by a physician who has worked with all the professional sports teams in Denver, so I was extremely lucky from that aspect – despite his less than stellar interpersonal skills. The pain medication dosage was too high for my size, and I ended up in the ER a week later with complications. Let's just say that a catheter is almost as bad as a fractured patella!

For the first time in my life, I knew I was "clinically depressed," as my leg was immobilized for seven weeks while my kneecap healed. I was horribly uncomfortable, in constant pain, and lacked my daily endorphins from working out. I completely recognized all this, but I made the mistake of reading horror stories on the Internet of people who remained crippled years after the same injury. I got out on my trails with the crutches, and I must have looked pathetic. I remembered lying in the mud where I had pondered what it was I was supposed to learn. I have never been a patient person, and I came to accept this negative attribute. I was indeed learning to be more patient, more empathetic, and especially more appreciative of my wife and children.

I had always been grateful when getting to the top of mountains because I knew that not everyone could physically climb to appreciate the feat and view. I quickly learned to become grateful for simply walking without a limp and not feeling like my knee was constantly on fire. I learned that in the big scheme of things, circumstances can change in an instant. As a self-reliant soul, I learned that I could (and did) become completely dependent on other people for mobility. My definition of self-reliance began to take on a new meaning. My "network" was not just about business contacts, but also about emotional connections. I realized as I started riding again with a number of friends that I needed them more for emotional, spiritual, and intellectual growth than riding companions. These were things I knew but had not really internalized. I had heard others say that an illness or injury could actually be a blessing. I didn't buy into this, but as I reflect back on my experience, it was an event that shaped who I am today.

There are many injuries and illnesses that are far worse, and I am grateful for my injury being relatively minor. I would never wish to repeat the ordeal, but it is something that caused a great deal of personal adversity because a big part of my identity is wrapped in the form of perpetual motion, fitness, and wilderness solitude. This event has served as a pivotal event in my life and a source of strength, resolve, and optimism.

A plethora of new research is demonstrating that developing an optimistic outlook and approach can be a learned behavior that has benefits for your health far beyond leadership. One such study by Toshihiko Maruta, M.D., a psychiatrist at Mayo Clinic in Rochester, Minnesota, looked at people in 1994 who had taken the Minnesota Multiphasic Personality Inventory (MMPI) at the Mayo Clinic between 1962 and 1965. The 500-question personality test had an optimism-pessimism scale that graded the "explanatory style" of the participants. Maruta found, "It confirmed our common-sense belief. It tells us that mind and body are linked and that attitude has an impact on the final outcome – death." He went on to say that optimists might be less likely to develop "learned helplessness," which to me is the polar opposite of self-reliance.

Even more inspiring, researchers believe we can do something about our own optimism and happiness. Richard Davidson, a neuroscientist at the University of Wisconsin, studied Buddhist monks who had extensive experience and training with intense meditation. Davidson sought to determine whether mental training for "compassion" could produce changes that produce happiness. Davidson found that methodical meditation could actually change neural pathways (he calls this *neuroplasticity*). In other words, each of us has the potential for our own minds to change the wiring of our own brain. Retired general Colin Powell said it another way: "Perpetual optimism is a force multiplier."

Take Away

Becoming an effective leader starts with a passion to enhance the human condition and the realization that you can't go it alone. Developing effective leadership skills is the desire to understand others and your effect on them. Human interaction is not like a science experiment with controlled conditions and repeatable results. Interactions and interventions amount to infinite possibilities. Every day, every person and every situation is nuanced in some intricate and fascinating circumstance. If the recipe existed, we would be able to test aptitude and leadership quotients and make effective leadership easily repeatable. But we can't. Since the beginning of recorded history, philosophers have opined about the dearth of leaders. What we can do is embrace the apprenticeship and become extraordinary learners who constantly and consistently study what works within the context of different events, different times, and different people.

Learning to lead boils down to focusing your time and managing how you respond to your environment. Your passion about a given undertaking and your attitude towards the people you lead must match your rhetoric.

Self-Reliant Leadership is synonymous with knowing which questions to ask yourself and having the courage to answer them and act.

What leadership experience taught you the most and why?

What knowledge and skills will you need to sharpen to become a more effective leader?

What can you do to make your optimism contagious?

Answering these questions will help you develop your leadership philosophy as a guidepost for future actions. Deciding when and in what future roles leadership is required to influence others is the important first step. With passion for a purpose, *how to lead* becomes a lifelong learning goal that is much more attainable.

> *Put more trust in nobility of character than in an oath.*
> —Solon, Greek statesman, lawmaker,
> and poe

Receiving my coveted Green Beret on
November 12, 1980 at Fort Bragg, NC.

Australian Rappelling as an instructor in 1981 at
Camp Mackall, NC.

Receiving my commission in April, 1984.

Wedding Day on July 1, 1984. To my right is George Callahan along with fellow soldiers from my Special Forces reserve unit.

A-Team in Bad Tolz, Germany in September 1984. I'm in the front row - second from the left.

In the middle - Bad Tolz, Germany in September 1984.

Sitting on the far left on my 66th military jump - July 1985.

Promotion to First Lieutenant, 1987.

My family in Kauai (June 2008). My wife Jacquie, daughter
Kristen, and son Kevin.

George Callahan holding the beret he presented to me
(May 2008).

Pinning my wings on my son's chest 30 years after I received them in the same place (August 2009).

My parents were on hand for the ceremony on November 12, 1980 at Fort Bragg, NC.

Chapter 7 – Conflicts and Dysfunction

Difficulties are meant to rouse, not discourage. The human spirit is to grow strong by conflict.
> –William Ellery Channing, early nineteenth century preacher

The greatest conflicts are not between two people but between one person and himself.
> –Garth Brooks, country music artist

Following my assignment as an instructor, medic, and sergeant, I left active duty and transferred to a Special Forces reserve unit in Tampa where I was simultaneously enrolled at the University of South Florida as a Reserve Officer Training Corps (ROTC) cadet. The simultaneous membership program, as it was called, prevented me from applying for an ROTC scholarship, but it did mean I would only have to be a cadet for two years before being commissioned as a second lieutenant. I was very cognizant of already being three years behind my contemporaries, having served as an enlisted soldier before going to college. Going this route to earn a commission meant I would become an officer at 22 – the same age as most people. I would end up completing college in three years, and being pretty competitive, I liked knowing I was really only one year behind my peers.

While in college, I had the extreme good fortune of being instructed and mentored by a young captain by the name of "Skip" Paul. He was a West Point graduate from 1977, the same year a huge cheating scandal occurred. The scandal crystallized Captain Paul's sense of ethical leadership. He was the rare individual you meet where you find yourself asking for years afterwards, "How would Captain Paul handle this situation?" Of all the people I have ever known, Captain Paul had the best internal compass for doing what was right and treating others as he would like to be treated. He had an easy smile, a strong military bearing, and he knew how to connect with people by somehow showing a twinge of vulnerability that commanded respect. He was a class act, and I am richer for having known him as a coach, teacher, and friend.

Captain Paul's ethical compass stood in sharp contrast to what I experienced at my reserve unit during monthly drills. Once a month, we would load a plane on a Friday night and jump into a drop zone somewhere in the Southeast. We would train all day Saturday and fly home Sunday. Many of the soldiers in the reserve unit were older Vietnam veterans and took the label "unconventional soldier" to a completely new level. For civilian jobs, most were blue-collar folks in government, law enforcement, and construction. There were a few lawyers and some mid-level executives, and the common ground was high intelligence and a general disdain for rules and authority. Little did I know I would experience in real time what I was learning in ROTC about ethics and common dilemmas for new officers.

The soldiers I served with had the highly desirable traits for deployment and combat but were highly questionable for a civilized society. Soon after I was commissioned a second lieutenant, I received a call from a team sergeant who was the ranking NCO on one of the top "A" teams in the battalion. He told me his team was headed to Maine for Winter Warfare training and needed an XO (executive officer). Serving as the company adjutant, I was flattered to be recognized for my leadership and jumped at the chance to command one-half of the "A" team. I also learned that I would have the chance to learn to ski, which was also quite appealing since I was a Florida boy. I remember thinking the team must recognize that I really did transition from being an NCO to a cadet to an officer in their eyes, and I felt a twinge of pride in my professional development.

To my pleasant surprise, the team sergeant told me that I really didn't need to do anything to prepare for our training mission and that he had everything covered. I thought it was nice to have dependable subordinates who could be trusted with delegated responsibilities. I was apprised to be at the Naval Air Station Jacksonville at a certain time with certain gear, and that's what I did. I was excited to "be a leader" with seasoned combat vets on a challenging training mission.

I expected to board a military transport plane with cargo-net seats and no windows, but I was amazed and impressed that we were boarding a small but plush plane. It was said to have been Lady Bird Johnson's plane, and I couldn't believe our good fortune. In our fatigues, we would fly from Florida to Maine in comfort. Upon boarding, the team sergeant produced a document to the Navy personnel, and I started to get the feeling something was amiss.

The trip was uneventful in that we were completely comfortable. Upon landing at the Naval Air Station in Brunswick, Maine, we were supplied with rental cars and billeted in NCO guest housing. As a new officer, I knew I wasn't supposed to be in NCO housing, but I went with the flow. I was told to pack civilian clothes so we wouldn't be conspicuous learning how to ski amongst the population. To my surprise, we didn't drive to an area to cross-country ski. Instead, we went to Mt. Abrams Ski Resort to learn to downhill ski. As a unit oriented to Eastern Europe, I was pretty sure that any combat missions would not involve chairlifts and downhill skiing.

It was sometime early that morning that I realized the team sergeant didn't have official orders for the trip and had gamed the system to make the trip a reality. I'm not sure if I mentioned that Special Forces soldiers can be extremely resourceful. I was so angry with myself for not knowing better. So here we were – a Florida "A" team that should have never been oriented to Winter Warfare training getting cold-weather training. We certainly weren't authorized for a trip that resembled a ski getaway more than military training. I had been duped into going, because I was the ranking scapegoat. Dumb lieutenant didn't know better, or sneaky lieutenant scammed the system … What would Captain Paul do? was my question.

The concept of balance came up yet again. Do what's right and ethical by stopping the trip and turning in the men, or let them know I didn't approve and maintain their twisted loyalty. Would they respect me more for doing what was right, or would they respect me more for conforming to the "norms" of a team that is expected to accomplish the mission no matter what? After all, we did have a military-trained locksmith and safecracker on the team and plenty of Vietnam vets who had the opposite of post-traumatic stress disorder (PTSD). In the end, I kept quiet because I was desperately seeking approval from men I respected. I didn't respect them for their ethical decision making but for their ingenuity to get some sort of winter training (albeit with a whole lot of fun) and knowing they would have my back if we ever deployed. It wasn't a matter of life or death, but it caused me to view the theory of situational leadership with a different perspective. Making ethical decisions is not always black-and-white, and the pros and cons aren't so obvious to young leaders when they're still trying to establish their core values.

I would be tested again, and this time in Germany. Like before, one of the top team sergeants in the unit approached me to be the executive officer on a deployment to Germany as part of an exercise designed to intimidate the Soviets, called *Reforger*. It coincided with the beginning of a school semester, but I jumped at the chance for a trip to Europe since I had never been before. Like the prior mission, I was honored to be the leader on a team who had scored higher than many active-duty teams on training exercises.

The team had a dynamic and charismatic captain and outstanding NCOs. I knew I was there because of rank, not experience or expertise. The mission called for the twelve-man "A" team to be divided in two, and I would be in command of half the team – five NCOs. Our mission was a "hide mission," which really meant strategic reconnaissance of "signature" vehicles that would indicate a significant shift of the enemy's strategy or a push into new terrain. The primary challenges with a "hide mission" involve navigating to the best location to observe, staying hidden, and communicating in short Morse Code bursts to prevent the enemy from locating our position via direction-finding capabilities. The hard part of the mission would again be dealing with those darn humans.

In a hide position, we had six men crammed into a glorified foxhole with debris covering the top. The primary challenge was preventing boredom by keeping the men awake and focused. To make matters more challenging, one of the soldiers on the team was Jewish and kept ranting about how all the elderly German people we were covertly observing were complicit in the Holocaust. In the course of a week, the men took to calling him "Murderer" because he became obsessed and a bit stir-crazy in the hide shelter. We kept him from acting out on his rants, and I knew that the way I handled the situation was closely observed by the other men.

At the time, I hadn't read about Shackelton's amazing survival story in Antarctica where twenty-eight men survived for almost two years without a single loss of life in 1914. But I did figure out that I also needed to keep certain men working in teams where their skills and personalities would mesh while also keeping them constantly busy with tasks. We had to encrypt and decrypt coded messages, which were like puzzles, so I put the brainiacs on that task. We also had to secure water, keep moving our latrine, and constantly repair our hide shelter, so I employed the more restless men for those tasks. For the mischievous soldiers, I had them forage at night for potatoes and other nearby "produce." It was an experience where I first learned it's far easier to prevent conflicts and dysfunction than it is to manage after it's had a chance to fester.

After completing my degree, I went back on active duty, but this time as an officer. After a military intelligence basic course, and much to my dismay, I found myself in a gung-ho infantry division in California. My preference would have been to stay in Special Forces, but I had since married, and constant six- to twelve-month deployments no longer held the same appeal. I was hoping for a strategic intelligence job in Washington, D.C., but found that aspiration was quite naïve – in ways I was about to find out the hard way.

As a new lieutenant, I did a pretty dumb thing (oxymoronic on a number of levels, for sure). After graduating from the officer basic course, I reported to my new infantry unit in my dress green uniform. I took the time to make sure my shoes were shined, uniform pressed, and brass polished. However, I forgot the most important thing: It wasn't about me shining. I needed to make a good impression with the colonel, demonstrating that my primary goal was to fit in and make his unit shine. I assumed that as a former Special Forces soldier, I would be automatically accepted. When I met the colonel, the first thing he asked me was, "When are you going to Ranger School, lieutenant?" With complete bravado and a touch of contempt, I said, "Sir, why would I do that? I'm Special Forces-qualified – *been there, done that*." My response invoked dead silence from the colonel and a look that could kill. It was the beginning of my end in that unit.

I didn't like him and he didn't like me, and it happened in an instant. What I failed to realize was that he had a lot of power over me. He was truly an egotistical and unethical jerk, but he was still my boss. I pushed for a lot of change in the battalion, and in the seven months I spent there, I accomplished nothing extraordinary. The executive officer pulled me aside once and told me to stop being Don Quixote. I was so unworldly that I had to ask what he meant. He told me all the change I was pushing for was like chasing windmills. It was then that I realized how futile my efforts had been, and it was shocking to realize (and admit) that I had failed.

I had never failed from a work perspective, and I blamed the colonel. I learned about adaptation and change through the school of hard knocks. I was the one who had to adjust to the cast of characters I would come across in all future endeavors. I certainly couldn't start with the mindset that others have to change as a tenet of leadership and a determinant of success. I had to change myself in order to influence others and make a difference. Later, I took responsibility for not handling the situation better because the thing I could have controlled was how I responded to my environment – situations and people. I hadn't yet learned which questions to ask myself, nor did I have the courage to honestly answer them and act. I was ultimately transferred up to the brigade headquarters (a promotion in a sense), and the departure was mutually orchestrated.

I have often thought about the world-renowned mountain climbing Sherpas of Nepal. The Sherpas are climbing guides known for dependable self-reliance, and they routinely carry an astonishing 93 percent of their weight! A key determinant of their success is a principle of physics referred to as the power-to-weight ratio. The concept implies that those with more power and less weight will find ascending easier. Leading oneself has similarities: I think of power as *desire and determination* and weight as *self-doubt, selfishness, insecurity, procrastination, and other bad habits.* There are three simple ways to improve the ratio: increase desire (which without action is a dream), minimize bad habits, or develop new habits.

I hated my job working for the battalion commander and rated it down with working like a serf at a plant nursery during college. It was repressive, and it was not the assignment I wanted as an intelligence officer. I was a staff officer, and I wasn't a platoon leader working with soldiers. I vowed to have more control in the future and to only pursue paths where I had a passion and could envision pouring myself into the work. I knew that passion went hand-in-hand with focus, and in this particular case, passion was the missing element.

I spent a lot of time deciding what my life would be about (and still do) and eventually realized that passion towards intense meaning would require *me* to change. I studied successful people, looking for the secret ingredient to emulate. What I observed is that highly successful leaders have a passion and focus for something, and they're willing to sacrifice something and delay comfort and enjoyment. Some people term this passion as hunger, and others have described it as persistence and determination.

When it comes to leadership, the examples cited above (where I made mistakes) basically involved misaligned expectations – expectations that could have been aligned had there been mutual trust, communication with candid assessments, and frank feedback. Communication problems often stem from misaligned expectations, and being transparent when it comes to balancing rewards and reparation is the best way to align expectations and facilitate healthy communication.

Leaders will always encounter disruptive and negative individuals, and like bad apples, they can sour the entire team. When there is poor morale and high turnover, it can almost always be traced back to misaligned expectations due to failed communications. This creates a dysfunctional team. When the five coaching steps are methodically followed, the opportunity to align expectations and improve communications is greatly enhanced.

For any organizational position, the people who support your leadership position need clear and concise job descriptions with enough detail so roles and responsibilities are clearly understood and acknowledged. The coaching sessions and formal appraisals that follow need to be consistent with what was initially outlined as the expectation. Updating, revising, and keeping expectations completely aligned is a balancing act that requires attention and a commitment to act rather than waiting in vain for the situation to improve on its own.

Take Away

After every exchange with the people you work with, ask yourself, "As a result of this interaction, am I exerting influence, and in what way? Am I viewed as an adversary or an ally for the people who depend on me?" Stephen Covey, author of "The Seven Habits of Highly Effective People," says we have accounts with other people, and that with every interaction we either make a deposit or we make a withdrawal. The language of leadership needs to be *clear*, *respectful*, and *congruent*. *Clear* language reduces ambiguity and aligns expectations (the greatest threat to communication failures). It is very difficult to become an effective leader without being an effective communicator (which is much different than being an effective speaker). *Respectful* language is the basis for trust and a collegial relationship. Language that is stimulating can also be motivating. We're naturally attracted to following optimists. *Congruent* language means the leader walks the talk – i.e., alignment between words and deeds, which leads to a model of integrity.

Warren Bennis, a pioneer of leadership studies, emphatically boiled leadership down to three basic tenets: Vision, Communication and Commitment. An effective leader can communicate a vision in a way that followers demonstrate a true commitment to the organization through their words and deeds.

Self-Reliant Leadership is synonymous with knowing which questions to ask yourself and having the courage to answer them and act.

Will people help you succeed? Why or why not?

What does reciprocity have to do with leadership?

What's the right balance of competition and cooperation to prevent dysfunction?

Buried in the setbacks and hard times are the seeds of future victories, if we're smart enough to look for them.
                    –Unknown

Chapter 8 – Building Teams

You must rouse into people's consciousness their own prudence and strength, if you want to raise their character.
—Marquis De Vauvenargues, French moralist

Behaving as and becoming an effective leader is a secondary by-product of an intense commitment to a purpose.
—James Clawson, author of "Level Three Leadership"

As a young army lieutenant, I regularly attended Officer Professional Development seminars with my colleagues. I always looked forward to these events, as they gave us a break from our troops, allowed us to bond with our peers, and helped us reflect on the bigger issues that were the foundation of every potential mission. One seminar in particular had a profound impact on me. The speaker was a retired Air Force colonel who would have made general had he not crossed into Cambodia during the Vietnam War to avenge his comrade's death. He spoke mostly about becoming a born-again Christian and what the experience taught him. One thing he said really stuck with me. "If you remember one thing about my war stories and lessons in leadership, remember this: All great men have kept journals." As examples, he pointed out past presidents, military leaders, poets, and other great influencers of humankind.

He went on to describe how a journal serves as a record of where you're at relative to goals. As discussed in chapter two, goals help you determine where you're going; how you plan to get there; whether you succeeded; and why or why not. The journal can contain the lessons needed for success if you have the *discipline* to openly and honestly capture your thoughts, ideas, experiences, feelings, frustrations, plans, and adaptations to those plans. I believe my personal concept of discipline and adaptability within the realm of self-reliance combined in a cacophony of emotion during that seminar: A journal is the ultimate self-coaching tool. Since that day, I have never traveled without a journal, and I hope that my leather-bound collection of *trials and tribulations* will be of some worth someday to my grandchildren. I often referred back to major decisions and stressful situations to see how I approached things. I looked at what I would have done differently and what I learned that altered my response to future similar and unique situations. Without those journals, I would have been relying on a fairly faulty memory.

I have not yet allowed anyone to read my journals, and I have stated (in the Irish brogue of my grandma), "They can only be read when I'm dead and gone!" My kids commonly joke that my chicken scratch is completely unreadable anyway and that the journals are most likely filled only with the musings of parental frustration based on misbehaved children years ago. They shall see ...

I have since read a bundle of books on leadership, served in many capacities as a leader, made a fair number of poor decisions, taught leadership to graduate students, and observed effective, ineffective, evil, and extraordinary leaders.

In the last chapter, I mentioned reporting to a colonel as a new lieutenant, but there's more to that story. Within a month of reporting to my new unit, we deployed to Panama to attend the Jungle Operation Training Center's warfare school. I was sick with bronchitis before we left, and my wife and I had just moved into a new apartment. After moving across the country, I was worried about leaving my wife in an apartment with a broken lock. I was miserable and sick with a poor attitude. To make matters worse, I neither liked nor respected my commander.

After a week of being in Panama, we had results of how the soldiers in the battalion were doing in the training. One of the generals was flying in for a briefing, and part of my job was to help prepare with flipcharts full of statistics. I carefully recorded all the scores – some good, some not so good – and taped them to the walls in the briefing room. The commander came in for the rehearsal, and in maniacal bravado started tearing down half the charts. Condescendingly, he said, "We need to accentuate the positive, lieutenant." I saw it as being completely dishonest, and I'm sure my feelings were displayed all over my face. I am not a good actor. Our platoon leaders were out in the jungle giving it their all to build teams and train soldiers. I believed an honest assessment for the general would help him see events as they were and provide appropriate coaching and feedback down the chain of the command. I thought the integrity would only help us improve our combat readiness. My thinking was idealistic and didn't consider the commander's career concerns. I did realize that leadership without solid core values stood no chance when it comes to the absolute trust needed from followers when faced with a crisis – for example, combat.

This was an eye-opening experience for me because I started to see a connection between the top of an organization and what that meant to the folks who actually do the work and carry out the mission. It made me wonder what sort of leadership strategy the general employed that he had a subordinate colonel who was afraid to be honest in reporting the status of training. What about the general's boss and further above in the chain of command? What happens when a lowly platoon leader hears about a less-than-honest commander – what does that mean *he* can get away with? What it meant to the organization's performance is that we had compliance but not true commitment. The junior officers delivered what the new commander wanted to hear, but they weren't committed to the man because his ideology and values represented only his own self-preservation. If we deployed and a small unit was hit hard, would he lie about the number killed or wounded and that a mission failed? Or would he wait to send in help, knowing that a failed mission would make him look bad?

It was an unpleasant experience to say the least, and I not only learned about Don Quixote, I learned about what type of leader I wanted to be. I knew I needed to really understand what my unwavering principles and values would be because leadership happens fast. There's often little time to reflect on every decision from an intellectual, moral, and ethical perspective. If I could work from a set of core values, the better my decision making would be, and in theory, that would help me earn the trust and respect from the people I would be charged with leading.

In my next assignment as the brigade assistant intelligence officer (S2), we deployed to Korea for an exercise called "Team Spirit." It was a year before the Seoul Olympics, and security was tight. Our primary mission was a show of force to North Korea and joint exercises with the South Korean military. The brigade commander was a colonel who was built like a bulldog. He wasn't much taller than me, and his cauliflower ears showed that he used to wrestle. He seemed to start a lot of the local races in Northern California, but we never saw him at the finish line. He used to fall out of unit runs, and back then, the leadership traits of endurance and stamina were linked to one's running prowess. In other words, the colonel, though older than his men, lost a great deal of respect. But unlike my last commander, I didn't question his integrity or his motives.

During one exercise, I remember briefing him about what I expected the enemy to do during the training exercises. I knew we had an exposed flank, and I predicted the brigade headquarters would be overrun if we didn't take appropriate measures. He sloughed off my recommendation, as if a military intelligence lieutenant couldn't possibly have the same instinct as an infantryman. As much as I hated getting woken up at three o'clock the next morning to move, it was good that in the dark, no one could see my smile when the headquarters was overrun. I had correctly predicted the avenue of attack and offensive tactics of the opposing force. It was training and not real, but it was good to be validated. The major I reported to told me the colonel would listen to me from now on. It was a good feeling, but I wanted the colonel to talk to me about his decision-making process; he was aloof, however, and that wasn't his style nor that of his generation. My boss did end up recommending me for an award and worded it in such a way that the colonel signed off on it, not knowing it was really an award for proving him wrong! Privately, my boss told me the award was for having the courage to recommend what was "right," despite knowing I hadn't earned the respect needed to put the colonel on the spot. What I learned is that my boss knew how to use the situation as a teaching opportunity and coached me all along the way. He put my growth and development ahead of his own agenda, and I appreciated how it made me feel. Over the years, I have always tried to lead knowing that if I help people get what they want, they'll help me get what I want – that is, a mission accomplished.

After being an assistant S2, I was selected to be a platoon leader in the military intelligence battalion that supported the infantry division. The colonel in charge of the battalion told me I was taking over a platoon that could only get better. With his stern look, I knew it was a team in bad shape – and an opportunity. I always thought it was a more invigorating challenge to improve a bad team than maintain a good one. It was a communications platoon within a military intelligence battalion, and unlike Special Forces, there were men *and* women. The colonel also told me the platoon leader I was replacing may have behaved "inappropriately" with the enlisted soldiers. I also had an assortment of soldiers with criminal records that involved violence, theft, and drug use. I was anxious to lead, but I remembered someone saying, "Be careful what you ask for, you just might get it!"

My platoon sergeant was a nice fellow, and literally and humorously, twice my size. He was not an effective leader because he wanted to be the soldiers' friend. I gave a speech at the first meeting with my platoon, and it was a speech I had rehearsed for years. What I remember was trying to frame expectations while letting the soldiers know I was not to be taken advantage of. I don't remember where this insecurity came from, but I did know that my ultimate job was twofold: Accomplish the mission if deployed while keeping the soldiers as safe as possible, and develop future leaders for the Army. I didn't like coming across paranoid, but given the background of the soldiers, I certainly was. I'm sure I thought the speech was inspirational at the time, but I suspect it did nothing to motivate a band of misfits. I approached the platoon from my Special Forces perspective of self-reliance and made no attempt to understand what the team's motivations were. I knew I was off to a shaky start because I was feared more than I was respected. When I entered the barracks in the morning, the soldiers would fall silent. I didn't have their trust or respect. I knew what was best for them because I was an officer – or so I thought.

What turned out to be difficult for me was that I couldn't understand why they weren't motivated, and I saw a complete lack of self-discipline and pride in their work. This was a foreign concept to me. Soldiers in Special Forces came from varied backgrounds (some also with criminal backgrounds), but they took pride in their work, and a "mission first" mindset existed. What was different here? Why was there apparent laziness with no pride? Why did the soldiers look for every loophole to escape work – work that was the training that would keep them alive in combat?

I had read all the small-unit leadership books, taken all the prerequisite leadership courses, and observed Medal of Honor leaders in action. Nothing I did seemed to be working to get my platoon functioning as a cohesive team ready for combat. I wrongly thought that if I provided better speeches, "my way" would sink in. I didn't know it, but I was appealing to an irrational mindset (I never thought about engaging soldiers from an emotional level). I'm sure I was initially perceived as a blowhard. I had wrongly assumed my enlisted time before becoming an officer would provide instant credibility and respect. I started to think that my platoon was a lost cause – soldiers to be feared in combat rather than relied upon. It's not good to worry more about your soldiers having live ammo and hand grenades than the enemy. I remembered that some lieutenants in Vietnam had been "fragged" by their own men.

A few months into my tenure, my platoon sergeant was replaced by a Vietnam veteran from Samoa. He was fantastic when we were in garrison versus field training and told me my primary job was in the field during exercises. He would take care of the day-to-day minutiae, and I would worry about leading the soldiers when we were doing what we were ultimately paid to do. What the new sergeant really taught me was that I needed to understand my place – my role as a leader. I needed my interactions with the platoon to be "measured." I needed to ration my time to enhance my impact. I needed to spend time thinking about what I wasn't going to do because overexposure actually detracted from my ability to be seen as the leader when it counted. If I worried about everything, the soldiers would not have a clear understanding of what really mattered to me and what it took to accomplish an objective. I needed to prioritize and focus on just a few things. I decided the top three things were training discipline regarding job skills; the ability to absolutely rely on each other (teamwork); and the endurance and stamina that only comes from a high level of physical fitness. This lesson of discerning activity from results has served me well, and in my opinion, this is a lesson many leaders frequently fail to heed.

Why do people choose to lead?

When new initiatives are started, the effective leader has to spend time deciding what will be discarded. It is the art of focus – as discussed in chapter five – the art of being true to the heart. After all, a leader cannot be all things to all people; this leads to confusion, failure, and a lack of clarity. Even the questions leaders ask convey insight as to what is an important priority. It's often said that you can't manage what you don't measure, but questioning everything ultimately means you lack focus on the important priorities for the team you lead.

Once I decided to focus on what really mattered, I found that my entry into the barracks each morning was not met with dead silence. My soldiers weren't intimidated by me and spoke more openly about issues that needed to be addressed. They weren't afraid to challenge me in a respectful manner. I also learned how to praise my team and worried less about being taken advantage of. I shed some insecurities, gained self-confidence, and was becoming more secure in my own role as their leader.

When I left my platoon, I was invited to the NCO Club for an informal going-away party. As an officer, it means a lot when your soldiers invite you to their turf. One of the sergeants made a brief speech and presented me with a simple plaque with the unit crest that read, "Good Luck, Sir." In front of the platoon at the NCO Club, he proclaimed, "Sir, when you rode in on your high horse, we didn't know what to make of you. But we have learned a lot and know you had our best interests in mind. We'll keep working on the things you taught us. We have become a better team and we're combat ready!" A few months later, the platoon deployed to Panama in 1989 to overthrow Manuel Noriega, and I took great satisfaction in knowing they performed extraordinarily and did not suffer a single casualty.

One of the things I enjoyed most about the military was how quickly a leader is able to assess his or her team. In the Army, deployments are common and usually involve some degree of suffering: sleep deprivation, hunger, extreme heat/cold, precipitation, fatigue, and the stress to accomplish the mission. In short order, these conditions allow the leader to see the character fortitude and flaws of individuals, who emerges as an informal leader, and the relative merits or dysfunction of a team. For most in the civilian world, the mundane day-to-day issues are only occasionally interspersed with the unavoidable episodes of crisis management. This can delay the learning of what sort of team you really have and what it means to be an optimist.

Leadership can take two tacks. One approach is that the leader initiates change without any external stimulation to alter and improve the organization. The other is when a crisis is thrust upon the person in a leadership position and tests him or her for all to see. The latter requires a different set of skills and the ability to see the situation, gather the facts, confront the realities, develop and test courses of action, and decisively move the organization beyond the crisis. In both instances, the leader must create a vision for the organization and articulate that vision in such a way that the team *willingly* commits and executes the strategy based on the leader's vision. The vision is the *why* that creates purpose and a sense of optimism for the team.

There is nothing that fear and hope does not permit men to do.

> —Marquis De Vauvenargues,
> French moralist

Leading is hard work. It is emotionally draining, mentally tasking, and physically exhausting. You will lose sleep over decisions before you make them and agonize afterward. You will struggle to balance the **tasks** to produce acceptable performance while maintaining the **relationships** in a way that gains commitment (versus compliance). It's tough work! A little too much *relationship* and you become a "buddy" to your team and struggle with *pleasing* while compromising performance. The antithesis, and equally detrimental tact, is to become a taskmaster. The autocratic leader will soon spend most of his or her time and resources recruiting and training. The team will either quit, or worse, perform poorly while engaging half-heartedly in key roles for the team.

It has been said that we become what we think about, and we get what we expect. Translated for leaders: You need a vision that comes from passion. You need to deeply yearn to accomplish something you can only do with the help and assistance of others who are equally committed. To gain willing followers, you need to reduce ambiguity with a clear vision, articulated and communicated passionately, in order to gain the commitment that's required for uncommon performance and mission accomplishment. Your success lies in knowing the difference between activity and real results. Achieving real results will require you to lead by example with an intense focus on four self-reliant fundamentals:

1. Know your own strengths and weaknesses.
2. Maintain strong and unwavering principles and beliefs.
3. Face change and uncertainty with confidence.
4. Make a commitment to continual learning.

I find it interesting to read obituaries of men and women who were considered extraordinary. Average citizens, as well as men and women of great fame and achievement, most often leave one impression on those they impact. My great-grandfather in Ireland was known for character, perfect posture, fine fiddling, and being a great carpenter. Ronald Reagan was known as the great communicator and for bringing an end to the Cold War. If a lifetime of activity and results can be summed up in one or two sentences, think about how a person's leadership can be summarized by the individuals who ultimately impact the organization and its success. There are tremendous distractions disguised as input when you lead, and the effective leader follows his or her vision while adhering to the four fundamentals listed above. Make it a habit to ask yourself daily whether your calendar is filled with activity, or if it's filled with items that advance your agenda to accomplish the results that will speak to your legacy. Every leadership position, no matter how small, leaves a legacy. To this day, I can tell you the strengths and weaknesses of every single boss I've had and the impact he or she has had on me.

Defining leadership is like defining many of the social science subjects. Every definition is open to critical debate, but the one that personally speaks to me is from James Clawson, a professor from the University of Virginia. *Leadership is the ability to influence people so that they respond willingly.* Personally, I like the fact that he included the word willingly because only willing followers are truly committed. Willing also implies an internal motivation. And the key ingredient in any relationship between people is trust, which can only develop when there is commitment and caring.

Take Away

Throughout my career, I have had the opportunity to coach people who are building teams. Listed below are the common themes I've heard:

How do I effectively challenge the status quo?

How am I supposed to do more with fewer people and fewer resources?

I wish there was a checklist to address tactical day-to-day leadership issues ...

I don't understand how so-and-so obtained so much power ...

I am on a dysfunctional team and I don't know how to fix it ...

I need practical advice, not theory, to drive change ...

I don't know if I am in the right place ...

I want a role that is personally fulfilling and that will be best achieved by making a difference in the lives of others ...

Much of the time, the folks asking these questions don't know where to turn. They have not tried in disciplined earnest to ask and answer the tough questions themselves. They have not been introspective and reviewed how past choices and decisions have led them to their present position where they are pondering why they are where they are. As has been repeated throughout, Self-Reliant Leadership is synonymous with knowing which questions to ask yourself and having the courage to answer them and act. There are plenty of self-help books out there, but many are written by academics, celebrities, or people analyzing the leadership secrets of some famous person in pompous prose that has no real-world application.

Based on my experiences, the three major characteristics of an effective team are shared accountability, a distinctive purpose, and real work. Is the accountability truly shared? Did you give up some measure of power and control so your team members are empowered beyond a doubt? Do team members know their distinctive purpose – where they're going and why? Does everyone have the same amount of work to do, and is the work aligned with your stated purpose – your vision? Was the team involved in defining the purpose? The key is shared accountability. Ask yourself again: Is your team truly committed to the purpose or merely compliant?

If you are the typical developing leader, you will likely have multiple roles in different organizations throughout your career. Many of the future opportunities available to you may not even exist yet. You can rest assured that leading people will never be something that can be automated, outsourced, or eliminated. With multiple roles in a myriad of organizations, you cannot completely rely on somebody or one organization to provide you with all the leadership development you will need to be successful. Nor can you necessarily expect an orderly career-progression path at one organization for your entire career. In simple, executable terms, you need to adapt and develop the discipline needed for your own personal growth and development as a leader and team builder.

While figuring out how to build a team to make a difference, how you approach your goals will be a key determinant of your success. Along with knowing where you want to go, you will need unbridled energy and enthusiasm, because optimism (or pessimism) is contagious. You'll also need an eye for the external environment for purposes of adaptation (i.e., course correction). Lastly, you will need a disciplined focus for your energy to ensure you make small steps daily towards your higher goals. Self-awareness and self-coaching are the catalysts for leading yourself, building your team, and motivating team members to new heights of accomplishment.

Self-Reliant Leadership is synonymous with knowing which questions to ask yourself and having the courage to answer them and act.

If you're a leader, you can't achieve your goals alone. Here is a concise but tough question that requires humbleness: *For whose good do I ultimately serve?*

How do you fix a dysfunctional team?

Are you investing in the professional development of your people? Are you helping them get what they want so they'll help you get what you want?

> *The speed of the boss is the speed of the team.*
> —Lee Iacocca, automotive businessman

Chapter 9 – Instigating Change

The Mirror

The good you find in others, is in you too.
The faults you find in others, are your faults as well.
After all, to recognize something you must know it.
The possibilities you see in others, are possible for you as well.
The beauty you see around you, is your beauty.
The world around you is a reflection, a mirror showing you the person you are.
To change your world, you must change yourself.
To blame and complain will only make matters worse.
Whatever you care about, is your responsibility.
What you see in others, shows you yourself.
See the best in others, and you will be your best.
Give to others, and you give to yourself.
Appreciate beauty, and you will be beautiful.
Admire creativity, and you will be creative.
Love, and you will be loved.
Seek to understand, and you will be understood.
Listen, and your voice will be heard.
Teach, and you will learn.
Show your best face to the mirror,
and you'll be happy with the face looking back at you.

~~ Author Unknown ~~

Leadership is nothing if not change. As leaders, we know affecting positive change starts within. We tend to think change is something we do rather than something we think.

Joining the Army was one of the biggest decisions I ever made, and it was something I decided on my own. Leaving the Army was an even bigger decision because I had a wife and daughter to support. The decision to leave the Army was a significant change because it required me to transform myself from a soldier to a civilian. Joining the Army at 17 meant I had literally grown up in the Army. Nine years later, at the age of 26, I was ready to instigate change for a new challenge. I had awareness that the military mindset was ingrained within me, and I knew the adaption and changes I needed to make would take a great deal of work.

The military taught me the value of backward planning, and with a firm departure date twelve months hence, I knew the exact day I needed to have a job in order to support my family. We were living paycheck to paycheck, and we couldn't afford to go a week without pay. We also had to plan a move from our post housing, where all the utilities were taken care of, to anywhere in the country. It was a year away, and I knew I had a lot of work to do. I made a checklist of everything I had to learn and accomplish and started envisioning what sort of job I would have. I knew I wanted to be an executive focused on big-picture strategy. I also knew I would first have to pay my dues in lower-level jobs. During a professional-development session for officers, a lieutenant once asked a general, "Sir, what's the best way to get where you are and earn our stars?" The general replied, "The answer is quite simple. Be a great lieutenant. Then be a great captain. Then be a great major.

Then be a great colonel. Simple. Focus on your current job, not the next one." I planned to take the general's advice and apply it in the business world.

I was fortunate to find a firm that specialized in helping junior officers transition from the military to the business world. The company made its money by receiving placement fees. It was in the company's best interest to help lieutenants and captains smoothly transition by cutting the military lingo from everyday vocabulary and resumes. In addition, we were put through mock interviews, we received a stack of business books to read, and we were given thought-provoking self-assessment assignments. Having majored in political science, I had a lot to learn, as most of the jobs available either involved business-to-business selling or manufacturing management. I didn't see myself working in a factory, and I knew a lot of executives started their careers "carrying the bag" as a salesperson and learning about the product, the customers, and the market. Selling also involves persuading people and marshalling internal resources, and I thought there were a lot of parallels to that of an intelligence officer. I knew I had to be involved in something I saw as altruistic, and with a medical background, I chose healthcare as my new industry.

I literally went to school on business. I don't think I ever really studied before, but I had an intense desire to advance my family's station in life and provide a better future for us. I was leaving the military behind and knew that what I was about to do was where I would invest my efforts to create a career. I also knew it would be hypercompetitive but in a different way than Special Forces. In the Army, it was all about the team, and in business, I heard that many people were more self-centered than self-reliant. The change I commenced was literally reprogramming everything about me.

As a lesson in leadership, I paid close attention to what worked for me when it came to successfully *navigating* change. Any Boy Scout remembers to *be prepared* and the role the "Ten

Essentials" serve as part of an outdoor creed and checklist for safe passage through the woods of any eventuality.

1. Compass
2. Map
3. Headlamp/Flashlight
4. Fire Starter
5. First Aid Kit
6. Extra Clothes
7. Extra Food and Water
8. Matches
9. Knife
10. Sun Protection

Whereas managers become skilled at and accustomed to taking the well-worn path, leaders emerge and exist to create new ones. Forging new trails means creating new directions. Given the relative discomfort with breaking new ground, it's important for leaders to understand how to get others to willingly commit to the new course through trust and predictability.

Listed below are the **Ten *Self-Reliant Leadership* Essentials** I believe it takes to affect change – first in yourself and then in others.

1. Passion

Your passion serves as an internal ***Compass*** and helps establish direction. Zeal for your mission/purpose begets commitment.

Do I have the hunger, drive, tenacity, persistence, and determination to realize my purpose?

2. Vision

Passion can be fleeting, so you need a vision that will sustain you when the going gets tough. Knowing where you're going is needed before you can convince others to willingly follow you to the destination. What you see as your vision also serves as the *Map* for others to "see" your destination.

Do I know where I am going and can I clearly articulate a destination that gets people excited enough so they will devote their discretionary time to reach it?

3. Consideration

Considering and contemplating all available options for a vision provides insight the same way a *Headlamp/Flashlight* illuminates what was previously unseen.

As I assess my vision, am I in the midst of gathering information, reflecting, assessing, and processing past events in my life to become an autodidact?

4. Intention

Intent ignites passion the same way a spark precedes a *Fire*. It's analogous to transposing thoughts into action. Clarify what's possible and what others can contribute.

What are the consequences of not changing (i.e., keeping the status quo), and what do I envision as a future state?

5. Planning

Planning is all about anticipating alternatives, just as packing a *First Aid Kit* is a thoughtful contingency for any venture. It's the "how" and the execution part of how you'll get to the desired destination. You know more than you think you know, and the people you lead need to know there is order, discipline, and purpose in your plans.

There's only one requirement here: Have I recorded milestones with due dates? The milestones include <u>who</u> does <u>what</u> by <u>when</u> and is central to diligent time management.

6. Commitment

Commitment is defined as the act of binding yourself (intellectually and emotionally) to a course of action. Packing **Extra Clothing** for an outing in the woods means you're determined and committed to the journey, and no matter what's thrown at you from a weather perspective, you'll persevere. An unwavering commitment is drawn from an intense purpose and optimism that results from a true leader, opposed to a person's role or position.

Is my passion a powerful desire that I translate into action?

7. Sacrifice

In my mind, there is no single trait that's a more important determinant of leadership success than the ability to unreservedly sacrifice in order to achieve deliberate outcomes for the greater good.

The act of bringing along **Extra Food** on a hike means you're carrying extra weight and have as a contingency the knowledge that current provisions could run dry. It means knowing that whatever discomforts you'll experience, the destination will be worthwhile. Surely you've passed people on an out-and-back trail who've said, "Keep going, the view is worth it!" Sacrifice is akin to giving up something in the short term in order to focus on the task at hand to achieve longer-term objectives.

The act of losing or surrendering something by sacrifice is the most important aspect of change for an individual or a team. Only through an intense desire to prefer the altered state will someone be ready to give up something. This mindset is why communicating a vision in a powerful way is so important to start the process of change. When people sacrifice something important, like precious time, only then are they ready to start to bring new ways to do things into the picture. Mutual sacrifice is a trust multiplier.

Think about what long-term substantive change means for your personal and professional life. Chances are, you are comfortable. Change from the status quo requires some level of discomfort, and as humans, we are geared to conserve energy. It might be cliché, but great achievements require great sacrifices, and mustering the energy required to begin can often seem daunting.

If I start something, what will I need to stop doing (e.g., time wasters)? Am I willing to make a sacrifice and leave my comfort zone to advance my own agenda?

8. Discipline

It's hard to sacrifice anything without self-discipline, much less sustain momentum towards a goal. *Matches* are essential to start a fire and provide a sense of security, just as discipline is required for a desired outcome to be achieved. There was a famous "marshmallow" study of children in 1970 by psychologist, Walter Mischel. The study showed self-control is reflective of better socials skills and a determinant of higher college-completion rates and incomes.

Can I stick with it, focus, and maintain consistency while avoiding procrastination? Does my behavior demonstrate uncanny persistence and determination?

9. Action

Before a *Knife* is used to cut, the user envisions what the knife will help create or alter. Action is the tool that follows intent and planning. The sharper the knife the easier the cutting, and the more focused the action, the greater chance for momentum and achievement. As the famous Greek philosopher Aristotle astutely observed, "We acquire virtues by first having put them into action." And Thomas Jefferson said, "Do you want to know who you are? Don't ask. Act! Action will delineate and define you."

Am I working my plan and hitting the milestones? Am I measuring success and setbacks so I can make necessary adjustments?

10. Habit

A result of repeated sacrifice, discipline, and action is something analogous to a routine. Just as you know *Sun Protection* can prevent painful sunburn in the short run and prevent cancer in the long run, you're also aware that good habits have short- and long-term benefits. Predictability creates trust in others, which is a result and benefit of discipline and sacrifice.

Has the new behavior become a habit where it no longer feels like a sacrifice?

The last marker of personal change is not so much an action, but a result of a disciplined approach to the ten steps outlined above:

Character (moral fiber) is built through the process of making a positive difference in the lives of others.

Has the habit become so ingrained as to become part of who I am? What will be my legacy with the people I lead? What can I do to augment my personal growth?

Look again at the ten steps outlined above. Think about where you have been an effective change agent. Which step is your strength? Which step most needs your focus in order to adapt the way you think, approach others, and truly affect change? Now think about something you've tried to change within yourself or as the leader of a team. To which step above do you most attribute your success? Is there a pattern for past failures – a step that tripped you up?

It's been said that if you need to get something done, ask a busy person, and if you're reading this, you're probably that type of person. Your plate is probably more than full with goals and aspirations. Think hard about what sacrifice means. Now think about what sacrifice requires. It means giving up something so you can focus. However, that's extremely hard to do. How often do you take on more and more and still expect stellar results? Leaders do the same thing with teams in their organizations and can't figure out why so many change efforts fail. To focus, you have to prioritize, and to prioritize you have to say no to things as an individual and as a leader, which may be the hardest step of all.

Uncovering your passion will provide focus for a particular starting point to serve. Knowing the cause to make a difference will help determine where you will need help from others. By being honest with yourself about your strengths and weaknesses, you will know where others can (and must) complement your own efforts. But keep in mind, very few followers will possess your passion.

Think about the people you most admire. Chances are very good they faced, embraced, and adapted to overcome some type of adversity while departing from a zone of comfort. Now think about how this applies to your desire to lead change with others. Is your passion connected to adversity you faced where you can help ameliorate that same obstacle for others?

Take Away

Only after you know yourself and the struggle to face your own hypocrisy can you start to affect change in others. Changing a team boils down to creating a compelling vision and communicating it in such a way that you gain willing commitment from those who will help you achieve your vision.

Communicating your vision requires a passionate (not necessarily perfect) delivery conveyed with a sense of urgency. The circumstances in which your vision is communicated can also affect the receptivity. Is there a crisis you need to overcome? Are your goals lofty and do they demand unparalleled accountability? Is there bad news and a scarcity of available resources? Should your vision be idealistic or realistic? Can you convey your vision in the form of a story with a beginning, middle, and elucidatory ending?

Gaining a true commitment versus acquiring mere compliance ultimately means empowering others. Empowering is a common buzzword carelessly used, as it actually mandates the leader to relinquish power. This requires a leader to willingly assume risk by allowing subordinates to make mistakes and falter, but it can help build a strong coalition. Be magnanimous. Participative planning helps create aligned expectations, and role modeling yields disciplined habits that will help produce desired results.

Self-Reliant Leadership is synonymous with knowing which questions to ask yourself and having the courage to answer them and act.

When will you decide to make a change in your current situation, and what sacrifices will you need to make on a daily basis to make that change?

What will you be able to do immediately to lead change in your organization?

What are the top priorities needed to instigate change across multiple generations?

> *If we don't change direction soon, we'll end up where we're going.*
> —"Professor" Irwin Corey, comic

> *It takes a l-o-n-g time to achieve change, but it takes forever to maintain change.*
> —Tom Peters, writer on business management practices

> *It is a secret both in nature and state, that it is safer to change many things than one.*
> —Sir Francis Bacon, English philosopher, statesman, scientist, lawyer, jurist, author, and pioneer of the scientific method

Chapter 10 – Continuous Learning

No one can give you better advice than yourself.
> –Marcus Tullius Cicero, Roman
> philosopher, statesman, lawyer,
> political theorist

Why did I have to learn most lessons the hard way? Probably because I was stubborn and ignored disconfirming information. If you don't learn from your mistakes, you're apt to repeat them until you do. I know I have! Successful leaders have the ability to know where they belong and where they can apply their strengths to succeed. I have had the very good fortune of working with leaders who were mentors and observing leaders who were god-awful. The ability to identify and attract quality mentors is a skill that provides an extraordinary advantage for learning to lead. I can always tell when I meet someone who wasn't mentored early in his or her career, and with job changes becoming more and more frequent, the ability to attract mentors will be a critical success factor for aspiring leaders.

Besides the leaders previously mentioned, I had one particularly outstanding post-military mentor. Two days after leaving the Army, he was the very first person I met at the company. I was leaning against a wall during a reception feeling completely out of place. On Friday, I finished out-processing the Army, and on Sunday evening, I was in Irvine, California. I was at a swanky hotel in a room of outgoing, confident, and well-heeled business people. My future boss saw me standing there like a misfit and took it upon himself to make an introduction. It turned out he was just as polished as everyone else, but he was also a good ol' boy from North Carolina. He was focused on being interested versus interesting, and I had never met a better listener – certainly not in the Army. He was engaging, funny, and had a sincere laugh that came from a truly humble soul. He quickly learned that I had served in Special Forces, and unlike most civilians back then, he seemed genuinely impressed. When he asked about the year I went through training, I told him about phase one in February 1980. He said, "That was one of the coldest months on record – I remember the blizzards!" With that, we were friends for life – we had a shared sense of suffering

Six years after that meeting, he would hire me as one of his managers, and that's when I really saw what emotional intelligence looked like. What made him great was his ability to ask questions that elicited deep thought and helped him provide direction without "telling."

As a new manager, the individuals I inherited were producing adequate results. At the same time, there were a number of personality conflicts that made the team highly dysfunctional. The personalities were the symptom, and the root causes were in line with what business consultant Patrick Lencioni notably described as team dysfunctions: *Absence of Trust, Fear of Conflict, Lack of Commitment, Avoidance of Accountability, and Inattention to Results.*

The team needed to work together to compete in an increasingly complex and codependent business environment, but it first needed to simply get along. I knew becoming an effective change agent would be difficult, but I also knew that it's the essence of leadership – and what was expected of me. Again, I thought I could simply rationalize my team into acceptable and positive behavior. What I failed to realize at the time was that there were multiple cultural, generational, educational, and socioeconomic dynamics at play.

My new boss parlayed his interpersonal skills and extraordinary method of coaching to help me learn to be a better leader. Many new managers use "techniques" to illicit the right responses from followers with such drivel as, "If I hear what you're saying ..." and constantly repeating one's name. This comes off as "techniquey," superficial, fake, and insincere. My mentor had perfected his coaching approach because when he asked questions, he genuinely cared about the responses he elicited. He always joked that he grew up in "Mayberry" because he was from a small town. He must have fine-tuned his small talk in that old-fashioned town. He didn't simply wait for his turn to talk but wanted to delve into what I was thinking and *why* I was contemplating various courses of action. He wanted to help me make better decisions. His line of questioning was profound and uncovered baseless assumptions, biases, and naiveté. He was also secure enough to let me stumble. He could accept small setbacks in *his* overall performance in order to develop leaders (and results) for the long haul.

Under his guidance, with a very diverse team, I was struggling with evaluating the team's strengths and weaknesses to improve the overall results. I wanted to achieve the overall goals, but I also believed that if I helped people get what they wanted (e.g., awards, promotions, etc.), they would help me get what I wanted (i.e., results and respect). I had a particularly bright and articulate man working for me who was very ambitious. He and I had a lot in common, but he was introverted and seen by his teammates as a brownnoser. I thought I had taken in all the relevant facts when I recommended him for a promotion, but my boss spent two hours at a donut shop asking me a series of never-ending "why" questions. During our intense discussion, my boss never offered his own opinion, nor did he tell me what I should or shouldn't do. He simply asked me questions that led me to take a step back and analyze the situation from a different perspective. He asked me, "Why do you think this person is ready for promotion? What behaviors have you observed that tell you he has leadership potential? What do his peers think of him – and why? What do you want your legacy to be with these people? Do you think your team is compliant or committed to the vision you outlined?" What occurred was a logical, rational, and thorough analysis of a leadership decision. I came away feeling very confident in my final decision as opposed to the indecisive state I was in prior to the meeting. I knew we mutually agreed when I saw that Mayberry grin, that ear-to-ear smile, when I summarized my new conclusion and altered course of action.

My boss didn't just help me make a great decision, he taught me two valuable lessons: Asking questions is a powerful leadership tool, and the listener really is the one with the power. He also taught me that taking time to formulate questions *you need to ask yourself* is one of the most valuable and oft-overlooked tools available. Susan Scott, author of "Fierce Conversations," wrote, "The quality of our lives is largely determined by the quality of the questions we ask – and the quality of our answers." The next time you find yourself in a personal crisis, brainstorm as many questions as possible. Think of aspects you believe are critical to determine if the right assumptions and contingencies have been addressed. You may be surprised how the insight helps you take a more measured approach. In fact, it will instill respect and confidence in your subordinate's perspective of your leadership abilities.

Because my boss cared, I wanted to exceed his expectations. Because I trusted him, I was always open and candid – even with my many shortcomings. Because he was committed to my success, I worked harder at tasks that I did not necessarily enjoy. To this day, he's one of the best leaders I have ever worked with. His effectiveness was based on his ability to actively listen, engage, and create willing followers. He didn't teach me facts or theory, but taught me to recognize patterns of behavior with others' values, beliefs, expectations, assumptions, motivators, and interests. He taught me *to teach is to learn*.

Because of this particular mentor, I have been much quicker to recognize when my values are in sync (or not) with those of my counterparts. That's what I learned from my experience. I had a better understanding of my own values, beliefs, expectations, assumptions, motivators, and interests and how my skills and experiences need to align with a team to make a difference.

Major General Perry M. Smith, USAF (Ret), wrote "Learning To Lead" and used the term "squint with their ears" to describe listening. He wrote, "The most important skill for leaders is listening. Introverts have a great edge, since they tend to listen quietly and usually don't suffer from being an 'interruptaholic.' Leaders should 'squint with their ears.' Too many bosses are thinking about what they will say next, rather than hearing what is being said now."

Your continuous learning can take place at work, on your own, or through charitable organizations. Your learning can take place anywhere you are able to work with others with similar convictions but where you are likely to have next to zero positional authority. The personalities in a charitable organization are more diverse than in traditional organizations where interview selection processes are inherently biased to keep teams homogenous.

Since leadership is part psychology, part sociology, part anthropology, part philosophy, and part political science, verbal communication skills and interpersonal skills are important determinants of effectiveness and success. Of course, there are traditional means by which to learn: seminars, courses, classes, tradeshows, lectures, journals, articles, magazines, and books. Perhaps you are reading this at the onset of new leadership responsibilities or before your first front-line supervisory role. A number of business schools now use case studies extensively to enable learning, and some are even adopting simulations and assessment tools to provide a true leadership experience along with peer feedback to increase self-awareness. You have the power to create the same experience for yourself in your current environment. Consider viewing your exploration into leadership as a case to become a student anew (i.e., a journey of learning rather than the elusive objective of obtaining "wisdom"). A learner mindset will require a steadfast commitment to enhance your experience, and the real challenge will be to develop candid channels for feedback on your progress.

If people really learned solely from reading, then the collective knowledge of leadership would have been distilled into evidence-based algorithms long ago, like the didactic approach of traditional scientists. Unfortunately, the research has not produced a definitive template for leadership development and success. The truth is, application of leadership theories and principles is still an art honed through emotional intelligence and displayed with interpersonal acumen.

Even when the best research is widely distributed within organizations, it does not directly correlate with better outcomes or the development of more effective leaders. The modern approach is to ask others for their secrets, and we continue to avoid creating and answering the tough questions for ourselves. Leadership has an infinite number of definitions and models, but the effective practice of leadership is an art – i.e., observable but unexplainable. Artists don't become masters by reading; they learn by observing, reflecting, and practicing – a lot. The emotional intelligence skills are the ones that will determine your leadership success by managing projects, visioning, or persuading – extraordinarily valuable but tremendously hard to learn.

Think about the challenges you have encountered thus far in your life and apply your own story to develop insights and leadership acumen for your future endeavors. The benefits of our collaboration are you will gain insight to develop new skills. You will lead with an appreciation of differing points of view, teamwork, the importance of lifelong learning, along with a true and ethical bearing.

The late, great management guru Peter F. Drucker once said, "We now accept the fact that learning is a lifelong process of keeping abreast of change. And the most pressing task is to teach people how to learn." He wrote a compelling argument for "managing oneself" and stated, "The most important event … is not technology, it is not the Internet, it is not e-commerce. For the first time – and I mean that literally – for the first time, substantial and rapidly growing numbers of people have choices. For the first time, they will have to manage themselves."

Leaders are readers, so don't stop your education now. Business guru Harvey MacKay penned an article titled "Learning Should be a Lifelong Endeavor" where he cited the following statistics:

If you read just one book per month for 12 straight months, you will be in the top 25 percentile of all intellectuals in the world.

If you read five books on one subject, you are one of the world's foremost leading authorities on the subject.

If you read just 15 minutes a day – every day, for one year – you can complete 20 books.

A great place to start the journey of self-discovery and self-awareness is to use a survey instrument (personality test) such as the Myers-Briggs Type Indicator® (MBTI). The MBTI describes sixteen basic personality modes and shows two opposing alternatives for each of the <u>four</u> orientations:

1. **E** for extraversion and **I** for introversion
   (*Energizing)*
2. Two choices for information uptake: **S** for sensing
   and **N** for intuition (*Attending*)
3. Two choices for judgment: **T** for thinking and **F** for
   feeling (*Deciding*)
4. Two choices for decision making: **J** for judgment
   and **P** for perception (*Living*)

Other personality traits, such as perfectionism and leadership, are derived from these four orientations, and we can each be described by a combination of these four letters. Each of the four scales of the MBTI (*Energizing, Attending, Deciding, and Living*) has opposing but complementary forces (i.e., the balance discussed previously). People are usually more dominant on one side of each of the four traits that creates the sixteen predominant personality combinations. All of us are made up of strengths and weaknesses. If you are action oriented, maybe you're not very patient. If you are detail oriented, perhaps you miss the big picture. Whether or not you use a survey instrument to gain insight into yourself, it's important to know how you are perceived by others and even more important to know how to best communicate to diverse personalities.

ProScan® is a similar survey that also measures energy levels, and it only takes five minutes to complete. It provides valuable insight into the team's satisfaction/morale and how adjustments they're making affect stress and energy levels. In addition, the ProScan survey is designed to be administered systematically as part of an ongoing leadership and management process. It measures the major aspects of self-perception, including an individual's basic behavior, reaction to environment, and predictable behavior. It classifies the following traits of human behavior into Dominance, Extroversion, Pace, Conformity, and Logic.

Perhaps you have already taken this test or another similar survey (e.g., DISC®, the True Colors Personality Test, etc.). What insight did the test provide? Are you Extraverted or Introverted; Sensing or Intuitive; Thinking or Feeling; Judging or Perceiving? People have great interest in these survey instruments because they focus on their favorite subject – themselves.

It is enlightening to take these tests. One can reflect on the accuracy and compare oneself to others. I would venture to say that if you have taken these tests, you found your results much more interesting than those of friends or colleagues. The real insight to be found in the tests is how best to communicate with other personalities. This is because personal effectiveness and leadership require outstanding communication skills. Did you change the way you interact with others as a result of taking the survey?

Empathy towards others is the part that requires the most attention but receives the least consideration. I also suspect that if an all-knowing person existed who could provide instant and accurate personalized insight, you would nary be surprised. You might find it fascinating that someone *gets* you. Why do we find it more interesting to find someone who *gets* us rather than attempt to be on the giving end?

Situations and circumstances can cause you to change and adapt in order to succeed and thrive in varied leadership situations. The situational leadership theory by Kenneth Blanchard and Paul Hersey presumes you must adapt in one of four ways to different circumstances and personalities to be effective as a leader. For example:

Directing *behavior is characterized by close supervision and one-way communication.*

Coaching *behavior is characterized by more two-way communication where decisions remain in the leader's purview.*

Supporting behavior is characterized by allowing the follower to control "how" tasks are accomplished and where the leader plays a facilitator role.

Delegating behavior is characterized by task control resting with the follower.

When you are aligned with work that best suits you, chances are you will feel energized and achieve greater job satisfaction. In other words, where there is *passion* and *satisfaction, achievement* and *success* will follow.

You are currently reading this sentence due to the sum of the choices you have made up to this point in your life. You might be thinking there were circumstances in your life that led you to this point, and I would say that might be true. At the same time, you decided how to respond to those circumstances and where you would spend your time from then until now.

Take Away

In the last chapter, we discussed instigating change. A motivator and humorist by the name of Charlie "Tremendous" Jones once said, "You are the same today as you'll be in five years except for two things, the books you read and the people you meet." I think that's a great quote, and I would add two things: You are the same today as you'll be tomorrow except for the books you read, the people you meet, the writing you do, and the sacrifices you make.

The process of writing, specifically journaling, teaches you how to think. It also provides insight with regard to understanding yourself, your surroundings, and how ultimate control comes from how you respond to other people. Writing also requires discipline, which is usually accompanied by some degree of sacrifice.

The Greek tragedian Aeschylus wrote, "He who learns

must suffer, and, even in our sleep, pain that cannot forget falls drop by drop upon the heart, and in our own despair, against our will, comes wisdom to us by the awful grace of God." He who learns achieves, and he who achieves must sacrifice short-term comfort for long-term gains. Successful leaders have the ability to know where they belong and where they can apply their strengths to succeed. The other thing about continuous learning is that if you don't learn from your mistakes, you're apt to repeat them until you do. Think about empowering yourself to start the lifelong journey of observation, persistence, humility and a disciplined approach to trial and lots of error.

Self-Reliant Leadership is synonymous with knowing which questions to ask yourself and having the courage to answer them and act.

What can you do to continuously improve your listening skills?

Why question answers rather than answer questions?

Based on your career aspirations, which leadership skills will you need that you don't currently possess, and how will you start to develop those skills today?

Consider asking people you admire and respect the following:

What was the best advice you ever received on leadership and why?

From a leadership perspective, who has most inspired you and why?

What leadership experience taught you the most and why?
What helped you early on?

What are the common mistakes and obstacles you wished you knew about?

What have you read that altered your perspectives?

If you had to give only one piece of advice to a leader, what would it be?

As for leadership, I see myself as a work in progress where I am more effective more often than I used to be, but not nearly what I hope to be.

Chapter 11 – The Ultimate Team

Leadership is not a matter of position; it's a passionate pursuit of purpose.

I started this book with a story about a boy in the wilderness who inspired me to become self-reliant. Over the years, I observed independent, assured, enterprising, resolute, and capable leaders. For me, the epitome of self-reliant leadership is a co-led journey that started in 1804 and afforded multiple lessons of commitment, discipline, sacrifice, courage, and stamina.

Successful journeys all start out the same way – a vision with detailed planning. Lewis and Clark co-led the ultimate team as the Corps of Discovery. The expedition was extraordinary in so many ways – not the least of which was extreme hardship, unspecified timeframes, and an unknown outcome.

President Thomas Jefferson created a vision for the journey through a very specific question:

Where is the United States with respect to fur trade, and is there a quick overland route to the Pacific?

Jefferson and Lewis rolled out a map, got on their hands and knees, and said,

We are here. This is what is known about the United States.

They made an assessment of where they were. There was no mistake about what was known and unknown at the time. Jefferson had just purchased a vast portion of the West that was rumored to contain volcanoes, wooly mammoths, and even the Lost Tribes of Israel. The second thing Jefferson and Lewis did was point at the area that was uncharted. Jefferson said to Lewis, "Your goal is to explore the Northwest Territory via the Missouri River, and find an overland route to the Columbia River and on into the Pacific Ocean." The direction Jefferson provided (oral and written) was crystal clear and focused on the *what* versus the *how*. The instructions Jefferson wrote for Lewis left no doubt what his objectives were. Lewis knew where he needed to go, what he needed to report, and what success looked like.

It was then left to Lewis to choose *how* to get there. He determined the structure, logistics, and most importantly, decided what type of men he needed on the expedition to be maximally effective and successful. First, he took ownership of the mission and responsibility for his own self-development. He sought advice from a number of experts in the fields of astronomy, navigation, botany, biology, geology, medicine, and ethnology. Columnist David Brooks wrote, "Wisdom begins with an awareness of our own ignorance." Lewis instinctively knew which questions to ask himself, and he had the courage to answer them and act.

Determining exactly how he would *get there* involved detailed planning and implementation, along with command and controls. One of the smartest decisions he is credited with in planning was asking William Clark to be his co-leader. Lewis knew his strengths, and he was acutely aware of his shortcomings. He knew Clark was better with people (emotional intelligence), and he made the unconventional decision to share leadership of the expedition.

How would he evaluate the success of the journey? His ultimate measurement was the successful exploration, mapping, and intelligence collection for his commander in chief. He spent over two years in the wilderness and brought back the information that was asked of him, only losing one man to appendicitis. It was clear where the mission started, how it concluded, and what the outcome would mean to the leaders, their men, and their country.

There has been a plethora of analysis on Lewis and Clark, and many others have written fine prose about the leadership nuances. For me, I learned you can't be afraid to get dirty – literally or figuratively. It's unlikely any of us are about to plan an overland excursion of uncharted wilderness, but you can still learn from the leaders of yore:

Where are you? Do you know your position on the map relative to your strengths and weaknesses?

Where are you going? Have you provided the direction your team needs to navigate successfully toward the goal you defined?

How will you get there? Are you focused on the *what* versus the *how*? Are you appropriately balancing the task at hand (mission) with the relationships of the team (empowerment)? What controls, measures, structure, processes, and incentives will you put in place to keep your expedition on course and focused?

It's a tough job. You can get your team lost – figuratively, of course. You can lose personnel and run out of supplies (resources) along the way. Pull out the map, get on your hands and knees, and plot your **location**, determine your **destination**, navigate with clear **direction**, and constantly **evaluate** the team's progress. But remember, the real learning will take place during your crucibles as your adversity quotient is tested. It's how you respond when you get lost, run out of supplies, lose people, forgo sleep, and make apparently mutinous decisions.

Take Away

Many people start careers with high hopes and then reflect on the fact that they're not living the life they envisioned. Ask them. Things are out of balance, and they complain about the status quo. They fail to try new things that will provide challenge and fulfillment. Odds are they achieved a certain level of comfort and stopped challenging themselves. They thought their education was complete when they received a piece of paper. Perhaps they gave in to self-doubt. Some of them believe they are powerless to the events around them, but a rarified few believe they are the masters of their destiny.

Leadership is an art, and your learning never ends. You must learn by doing and by watching the masters. Some guides are obvious. You can look to the history books and sports pages for examples that personally speak to you and help you relate your experiences to lessons of the past.

I took on the challenge to earn my private pilot's license and expected it to be a cakewalk. After all, I think I'm a great driver. Boy, was I overconfident! Learning to fly will challenge you mentally, physically, and emotionally. There was a lot to learn, and it was akin to graduate school from a studying perspective. Physically, it reminded me of drumming. I had to use one hand to control side-to-side and up-and-down direction, one hand to control the throttle, and my two feet to control the rudders (which I had trouble reaching). I had to listen to the control tower intently, precisely remember directions to communicate back concisely, listen to the wind sounds, and even use my sense of smell with regard to engine performance. Landing a plane forces you to intently focus and employ everything you've got to perform satisfactory. Pilots say a successful landing is one in which you walk away, and every landing I performed was different – with only a handful that I thought were "perfect."

What did I learn about leadership from flying? I relearned not to quit, and that anything worth achieving requires sacrifice. During my training I had a particularly bad landing in a crosswind where I failed to "crab" appropriately to keep the plane centered on the runway. After I landed, the wind pushed me to the side, and I failed to compensate. As a result, I went into the grass on the side of the runway. This is what I wrote in my journal that day:

The quote for today was as follows: *You may be disappointed if you fail, but you are doomed if you don't try.* Today was the worst. I had a good time in the practice area and was coming in for touch and goes. The tower cleared me to come straight to the numbers. I came in at a 45-degree angle, and just before touchdown, felt a crosswind from my right so I put in a little left rudder. I touched down pretty good but faster than normal, and the nosewheel didn't stay up as it should have. Before I knew it, I was rapidly drifting to the right and couldn't do anything about it. I can't remember what sort of control inputs I gave at that moment, but obviously they weren't right. I went off the runway and was glad I didn't flip. The tower yelled for me to STOP and not move. All I wanted to do was get back on the runway and get out of there. An operations vehicle came out, and the "incident" caused a temporary closure of the runway. I finally convinced ATC to let me taxi, and as I contacted ground control, the fire truck showed up. I taxied to the tie-down area (with the emergency vehicles in tow flashing their lights) and was met by my instructor and the flight school owner. I apologized and tried to figure out what happened. That's what bugs me – I don't know what I did wrong. I'll go back up with my instructor tomorrow. I apologized to the flight school owner, and he was really nice and tried to make me feel OK. Anyway, I feel like quitting, but know that quitting would leave me with a crappy sense of self-worth longer than this unfortunate incident.

As they say, you have to get back on the horse. I went back up the next day and afterwards wrote:

> Six landings with the instructor with a lot of attention to holding in the rudder control on the crosswind landing. I was also keeping the nose off the ground until the last seconds. I need to remember to reduce power when I start the level flight. One of my landings was very soft due to not taking the power out. Good lesson if it's ever rough and I want to "smoothen" the landing. Two landings solo and a real confidence boost. So far, 118 landings, 20.5 hours of dual, 6.5 hours of solo, and 27 total hours.

Like the Lewis and Clark expedition and the entire flying experience taught me that growth comes from pushing yourself and your team out of comfort zones. Leadership is an exciting endeavor and one that should be taken extremely seriously. You are empowered to make people better than they would be otherwise. You must first do no harm, but inaction is also a decision and can be just as unforgiving. Along the way, know that the best teacher is yourself – in the way you process your lessons.

Self-Reliant Leadership is synonymous with knowing which questions to ask yourself and having the courage to answer them and act.

How can you use daring goals to stretch people to do more than they think they can?

How do you guide people to the source of their own power?

What do you think of you as a boss?

Nothing is more difficult, and therefore more precious, than to be able to decide.

–Napoleon Bonaparte, French military
and political leader

Chapter 12 – Hear the Unheard

The Sound of the Forest[1]

Back in the third century A.D., the King Ts'ao sent his son, Prince T'ai, to the temple to study under the great master Pan Ku. Because Prince T'ai was to succeed his father as king, Pan Ku was to teach the boy the basics of being a good ruler. When the prince arrived at the temple, the master sent him alone to the Ming-Li Forest. After one year, the prince was to return to the temple to describe the sound of the forest.

When Prince T'ai returned, Pan Ku asked the boy to describe all that he could hear.

"Master," replied the prince,
"I could hear the cuckoos sing, the leaves rustle, the hummingbirds hum, the crickets chirp, the grass blow, the bees buzz, and the wind whisper and holler."

When the prince had finished, the master told him to go back to the forest to listen to what more he could hear. The prince was puzzled by the master's request. Had he not discerned every sound already?

---

1 Harvard Business Review, Sept. 18, 2003, "Parables of Leadership" by W. Chan Kim and Renee A. Mauborgne.

For days and nights on end, the young prince sat alone in the forest listening. But he heard no sounds other than those he had already heard. Then one morning, as the prince sat silently beneath the trees, he started to discern faint sounds unlike those he had ever heard before. The more acutely he listened, the clearer the sounds became. The feeling of enlightenment enveloped the boy.

"These must be the sounds the master wished me to discern," he reflected.

When Prince T'ai returned to the temple, the master asked him what more he had heard.

*"Master," responded the prince reverently, "when I listened most closely, I could **hear the unheard** — the sound of flowers opening, the sound of the sun warming the earth, and the sound of the grass drinking the morning dew."*

The master nodded approvingly.

"To hear the unheard," remarked Pan Ku, "is a necessary discipline to be a good ruler. For only when a ruler has learned to listen closely to the people's hearts, hearing their feelings uncommunicated, pains unexpressed, and complaints not spoken of, can he hope to inspire confidence in his people, understand when something is wrong, and meet the true needs of his citizens. The demise of states comes when leaders listen only to superficial words and do not penetrate deeply into the souls of the people to hear their true opinions, feelings, and desires."

With the cadence of a crisp military order, a young female cadet said, "New cadets, you have ninety seconds to say your goodbyes." With those words, my son realized his dream and started on his journey to become a military officer. At the end of that long summer day at West Point, the plebes marched out of famed sally ports and took their oath. The chaplain emphasized how significant their service and sacrifice was in a time of war. I choked up behind my sunglasses, thinking I was fooling my wife, my daughter, and myself. The chaplain rhetorically asked, "Who among these thousand cadets might be president? Two or three decades from now, time will tell …" In a flash, the ceremony was over and the cadets were marched into the giant arched doorway of Washington Hall. Thirteen hundred cadets were swallowed up inside with astonishing speed. Two thousand parents were standing on the famed plain parade field before the mammoth arched doors, mouths agape. After eighteen years of nurturing, there was no guidance, direction, instruction, or sympathy for giving a son or daughter to an institution. Some of the parents still had children at home, but some, like me, instantly became empty nesters. There would be no training, transition, or manual, but unbeknownst to me at the time, there would be yet another test.

Over the next nine months, I would struggle mightily. In fact, letting go of my son – giving my son to the service of our country – would be the hardest thing I had ever done. And I was utterly and completely unprepared. Perhaps if he wasn't a good kid or if he didn't share similar interests it would have been easier. He had made a game out of schooling me at chess since he was 6, and at 16, he would destroy me in all things physical. As we raised him and prepared him for leadership, I found that he was the one teaching *me*. We visited Normandy when he was 11, and he literally wept as we walked amongst the thousands of graves. That's when he taught me what honor really means. When he got hurt in sixth grade and couldn't play soccer, he switched to swimming. Despite being years behind kids who had swum competitively, he taught me about fortitude when he finished last in every race the first year. And in his absence he taught me another lesson – *hear the unheard*.

Hearing the unheard refers to a commitment to develop your communication skills by being observant, empathetic, and listening. It's a matter of self-reflection and self-discovery, along with accumulating expertise in the field in which you lead. The unheard is hearing your inner voice. It's about asking yourself hard questions and working long and hard on the answers. It is not about immediate answers.

To answer these questions, I knew I needed solitude to just think. I needed time to let the questions rattle around in my head and let the answers come on their own schedule. I knew the answers could not be forced. I took a month off where I sought solitude in nature. I backpacked the Colorado Trail, went on long bicycle rides, and traveled to the jungles of Costa Rica. This is where I could get away from technology and even airplane contrails. What I found surprising is that it was hard to concentrate on forming and developing the answers to the questions I needed to address. I would start to work through a question and my mind would wander to a plant, a bird, or even a cloud pattern. I couldn't believe that nature was so distracting! I came to realize that I had not yet relaxed and let go. I needed to really let go in order to hear the unheard. Once I did, the answers started to form. I wasn't in task mode anymore, and I (for once) felt "lazy." It was a curious feeling, but I didn't feel like doing anything but eating, sleeping, hiking, and watching wildlife.

It was while watching four carefree species of monkey troops pass through the trees near our cabana that I started to realize how out of kilter my priorities had become (me facing my own hypocrisy). When I realized how I had come up short in so many areas, I first examined my failings – the things that were truly under my control. There were a lot! It was overwhelming, until I grouped them into categories and realized they could be categorized under focus and patience. Focus and patience are interrelated because I need the patience to be focused, and staying focused requires patience. This seems clear-cut, but not for a guy who always believed the race is not always to the swift but to those who keep on running. In the noisy solitude of a Costa Rican jungle, and with ample time, I was finally forced away from the distractions that prevented me from hearing the unheard.

There are fifty-four mountains in Colorado that measure over 14,000 feet in height, and most of the ones I have climbed, I have climbed alone. On one particular climb, I had seven solitary hours to contemplate the oft-cited metaphor of mountain climbing and leadership.

The first thing I thought about while stressing and straining over the trail was, "Why am I doing this? What motivates me to push myself in sometimes tough conditions?"

I wasn't able to answer that question for myself until I reached the summit. I wondered if the altitude had something to do with it, but the higher I climbed, the more daily distractions faded away and I was able to focus and think. At the summit, I realized my little epiphany of why I climb is rather cliché: It makes me feel alive and purposeful.

I found the purposeful part odd, as solo climbing is a rather selfish pursuit. For me, climbing is central to my very being. It's like what reading is to my mind and exercise is to my body. I need to climb to be a (whole) better person.

Like every leadership assignment I have ever had, none of the mountains I have climbed were easy. Like the teams I've led, each mountain has its own personality – like the way the weather wraps around the mountain and the way routes seem to disappear in front of you. Just like leadership, where teams react positively or negatively to challenges, the outcome is not always predictable.

Some of the mountains I have climbed were more challenging than others. None were without their moments where I had to dig a little deeper than I thought I would – or could. Like life and leadership, there are plenty of external factors that are uncontrollable.

The weather determines the temperature, which determines the layers of clothing. The wind can make a tricky ridge even more difficult. Rain can make a trail a muddy and slippery mess, and snow can make a route hard to find. Just like leadership, the route requires adaptability and the self-reliance to persevere despite hardship.

Unlike leadership, climbing a mountain is temporary. Dedicating the better part of a day to a physical activity is easier than the stamina required to put forth your best efforts day after day in the pursuit of a vision.

The metaphors between climbing and leadership were most applicable if one was engaged in leadership while actually climbing the mountain. I met a woman on the descent who had been abandoned by her team, who summited without her. She seemed resigned to the fact that she wasn't strong that day, but not summiting with her friends will be with her forever. How sad it was that the team wasn't able to get everyone to the summit. It makes me wonder what the team dynamics were, who the leader was, and what the individual and group motivators were.

I also met a soldier on the mountain who had just returned from Afghanistan. In the brief five minutes we chatted, we didn't talk about the route, the summit, or the weather.

We talked about the team he led in war. Here we were in one of the most beautiful places in North America on a pristine day, and this soldier was talking about people rather than nature. I think I represented someone safe to speak with: I wasn't a fellow soldier, I wasn't his family, and I wasn't the press. He told me how he lost eight soldiers as a platoon leader while manning an indefensible base.

He cupped his hands and explained how they were placed in a bowl of mountains and were expected to defend it from an enemy that had the higher ground. It was heart wrenching. Here was a soldier who had just returned from combat, and the first thing he did was climb a mountain. I realized that climbing the mountain for him was a cleansing experience, a place to hear the unheard and renew.

For those of us who climb, the mountain serves as an anvil. The inertia of the mountain allows the energy of climbers to be transferred to their very core.

West Point would again serve as the learning ground to hear the unheard when I took a ride with the Army Cycling Team. I couldn't imagine a better opportunity to observe a collegiate team in action than to spend two hours riding with them. In fact, I can't imagine many college sports where someone of a certain age can intimately participate without risking serious bodily injury!

As we were preparing to ride, the team assembled in the basement of Cullum Hall – one of those ancient, granite fortresses along the Hudson River. The basement was pretty dingy and damp, but what I noticed most was how quiet the team was as we assembled on a cool autumn morning. The team came to work and approached their preparation very methodically. Pre-ride preparation means lowering the chance of mechanical failures, being properly fueled, and having the right layer of clothes to stay comfortable. This preparation is as much selfish as it is for the team. Getting stuck on the side of the road or falling off the back means the team waits, and that diminishes the training objective and effect.

As we started the ride, the team captain announced the

route – a two- hour ride with some hills. "Some hills" turned out to be nearly 2,000 feet of climbing. The team was outfitted in black and gold kits, and with great pride I rode off the post towards the hills with about fifteen of our nation's best and brightest. As we warmed up, the good-natured jokes started immediately. There was a quote from a British officer who recently visited West Point and told the cadets their institution was basically a "Mensa prison" disguised as a college. There were also announcements of nicknames and self-deprecating jokes that established the tenor of the ride and served to set performance expectations. In case I couldn't tell from body types, I got a quick rundown on the climbers, sprinters, and track racers. At the same time, the dynamics of the team came alive.

"Dynamic" can be characterized by energy, force, or power – especially one that motivates. And this team's dynamic was immediately on full display. To the untrained eye, cycling might not seem to be a team sport, but the physics of velocity deem tactics of strategic importance. The trash talk gave way as the slope of the road increased, and the physical leaders emerged as the pace increased. As the position of riders in the group ebbed and flowed, I realized the team had created equilibrium of competition and collaboration. The average rider on the team was about 20 years old, and somehow, two months into their training season, they had formed, stormed (I assume), normed, and were now performing quite well. For an institution known for its rigidity and hierarchy around command and control, I observed a very self-directed team.

The United States Military Academy often refers to its cadets as future leaders of America's sons and daughters. During the ride, I wondered what a business or nonprofit team could learn from these emerging leaders. For one, the tough selection process, especially in a time of war, means there is a tremendous amount of homogeneity not usually found in today's work teams. That's not what brought the team together.

Instead, I saw a shared sense of purpose, a common vision for the future, and a commitment to not let the team down. The cadets were truly giving a 100 percent effort. In essence, there was a shared objective, a shared commitment, and a shared sacrifice. The intrinsic reward was simply their place on the team and a sense of belonging. The only punishment I could envision was not meeting the team's expectations, which would result in the loss of respect amongst one's peers.

If your team can create a shared objective, you're halfway there. The other more difficult half is figuring out how to create a shared commitment with a corollary sacrifice. Getting buy-in on sacrifice is hard. It means giving something up (e.g., time, other projects, etc.), and that represents change – something most people abhor. Successful change occurs when motivations and rewards are aligned, and the inevitable "what's in it for me" is much harder to calibrate on a diverse team. As they might say at West Point, leadership is not for sissies, and the reward is in the privilege of belonging to something bigger than oneself.

Take Away

We all fear irrelevance. We all want to make a difference. We feel like we make a difference when we're around people who make us feel important. When you feel important, you work on things that make a difference in the lives of others. You must care deeply about people and believe that serving them serves a higher purpose; your passion and vision.

Leadership is exacting your will over others – getting people to do things they otherwise wouldn't. Most people never really want that. As a result, they must trust you. How do you earn trust? Truly care about your team. Commit to doing your best for your team. Be reliable and predictable. Does that just happen? No. You need character that is defined by integrity and courage. The key to character development is developing positive habits, and that comes from self-discipline and sacrifice. And it only makes sense to apply these traits in areas where you have passion. Apply that passion to acquire knowledge, develop skills, and gain experience. Once that's established and you are chosen to lead, your team will *willingly* follow. Leverage strengths and minimize weaknesses. Create a vision. Communicate steps to accomplish the vision, and always remember that simplicity is key.

What will be your legacy? Pause for a moment and reflect on your answer to this question. Think hard because your answer (or nonanswer) is likely to determine the direction you take yourself and others on the journey you are about to begin. Results are important, but remember that you need a true commitment from your team in order to sustain superior performance. Stay out front and lead by example. Don't ask your team to do anything you wouldn't do, and be guided by your own personal value system. It must be beyond reproach. All mistakes are forgivable except those involving integrity.

Self-Reliant Leadership is synonymous with knowing which questions to ask yourself and having the courage to answer them and act.

Are you moving deliberately with purpose? What will be your legacy?

How can you focus your energy to produce the greatest impact? Is your passion your life's work?

Is a good portion of your life dedicated to the service of others? Are you living a good life? What is a good life?

To create a leadership model for yourself, write down the challenges you're facing (or expect to face); the implications of the challenges you're facing (or expect to face); organizations you're leading (or expect to lead); core leadership principles you plan to adopt (and why); and ways in which you will improve your potential for leading change to improve the lives of others.

Listening, not imitation, may be the sincerest form of flattery.

> –Dr. Joyce Brothers, psychologist, television personality, and advice columnist

Epilogue

He who knows how to suffer everything can dare everything.
    –Marquis De Vauvenargues, French
    moralist

I had not planted my feet on that ground in thirty years, but there I was standing in front of 460 brand-new paratroopers at Fort Benning, Georgia. I remembered some aspects of my training clearly, but some of it was like looking through a screen door on a foggy day. Thirty years is a long time, and I wondered how that training had shaped who I had become. The NCO in charge of the graduation ceremony called out twenty-five students to assemble in front of the parents and grandparents who had earned their wings in years past. It was surreal as my son posted himself in front of me and I pinned the wings I earned in 1979 on his chest. Never then, nor recently, did I think I would have the honor and privilege. Seeing my son beam was much more gratifying than when I had earned the wings myself.

What struck me during the ceremony was that the soldiers I trained with at the height of the Cold War never thought we would fight the Soviet Union, so training always felt like drill. Fort Benning now has a palpable energy that did not exist in

1979. Back then, the only soldiers with combat patches on their right shoulder were "old" Vietnam veterans – soldiers we couldn't really relate to. Today, almost every soldier on the post has a combat patch indicating that he or she had recently deployed to Iraq or Afghanistan. What stands out to a casual observer is that these soldiers are astonishingly young. There is no doubt today's military training takes on special relevance and urgency in time of war, and these young men and women joined knowing the risks "without any mental reservation." In the 1980s, we learned skills but never had to test our will. Today, these soldiers know that their ability to persevere, their indomitable will, is principal to their success as leaders. Their fellow soldiers depend on them to survive and succeed in the harshest of circumstances.

Final Take Away

We are in desperate need of leaders. Maybe there's a school somewhere that chisels heroic figures, but I haven't seen it yet. As you scan our American landscape, you see "leaders" who spout whatever lines get the most applause. They fritter away precious time that should be spent solving our big problems – as they try to be sure they don't offend anyone.

Look at the leaders you read about in the paper; you can find some of them in prison or well on their way. The papers are full of people – often those we've elected to spend our tax money – who bribe, plagiarize, bend, or simply ignore the rules. I don't need to list every scandal because the media is full of them every day.

I'd like to suggest a solution. Picture someone running an organization. Imagine if that person always told the truth, if he or she always followed predicable and laudatory principles, believed in human dignity, and thought setting an example was paramount to earning respect and gaining trust. At this point in our history, wouldn't that be such a stunning even shocking thing to do? And wouldn't it be so incredibly welcome?

The way to get from here to there is to **become that person**. Maybe you aren't a leader right now. Maybe you've just begun your tentative steps in the world. I hope you have decided you want to lead and make a difference. My intent is to provide a new path with tools, ideas, and "essentials." Knowing which questions to ask yourself and accumulating knowledge about theory is the first step, but knowing how to apply that knowledge with people and situations is the art. Mastery of any art only comes from practice and experience. You need to stick your neck out.

If so, you are accepting a heavy burden and a privilege: Leading men and women to accomplish great things. A good leader remains a student of leadership and uses his or her acquired experiences to teach, coach, and inspire others to reach their potential. Learn to inspire yourself. Your leadership impact might influence only one person a little bit. At the same time, it could impact thousands.

No book can make you a leader. My aim is to show you how to be your own "leadership laboratory." Use what you have learned to speed up the learning process so you can learn your life lessons quickly. Challenge yourself to change and be open to more change. Accept and even welcome adversity because it will be your prime teacher.

I believe you have control over two things in your life: how you spend your time and how you choose to respond to your environment. If you do each well, and wisely, you will **become an extraordinary leader**. We need you.

Good luck navigating. I wish you a safe journey with a life of learning, teaching, and serving.

Decisions Determine Destiny

Final Note

In the span of a career, I spent a relatively short period of time in Special Forces: three on active duty of which half the time was training, and three years in a Special Forces reserve unit. All of my service occurred during peacetime, which is much different than an army at war. My relatively short time in Special Forces shaped me primarily because it took place at an impressionable time when I was literally becoming a man. There are multitudes of Special Forces soldiers that served before and after me that paid the ultimate sacrifice. Some of those heroes have been recognized as national treasures, and I make no claim whatsoever that I am one of them. I was fortunate to meet some phenomenal soldier leaders, and I remain an inspired lifelong student of leadership because of their example.

De Oppresso Liber.

Recommended Reading

"Undaunted Courage" by Stephen Ambrose

"The Social Animal: The Hidden Sources of Love, Character, and Achievement" by David Brooks

"Leadership: The Key Concepts" edited by Antonio Marturano and Jonathan Gosling

"The Future of Management" by Gary Hamel

"Switch: How to Change Things When Change Is Hard" by Chip & Dan Heath

"WAR" by Sebastian Junger

"When Pride Still Mattered: A Life of Vince Lombardi" by David Maraniss

"The Unforgiving Minute: A Soldier's Education" by Craig Mullaney

"Creating the Good Life: Applying Aristotle's Wisdom to Find Meaning and Happiness" by James O'Toole

"The Diary of a West Point Cadet" by Preston Pysh

"The Power Of Simplicity: A Management Guide to Cutting Through the Nonsense and Doing Things Right" by Jack Trout

About the Author

Jan Rutherford entered the U.S. Army at age 17. He spent six years in Special Forces as a medic and "A" team executive officer and three years as a military intelligence officer. Since then, Jan's business roles have been in the areas of sales management, corporate training, marketing, business development, product management, and government affairs.

Jan has taught leadership courses to graduate students at the University of Colorado and the University of Denver. He has worked with a number of charitable organizations and has also been a speaker at industry conferences in Europe and the United States.

Jan's free time is spent traveling with his wife, spending time with his adult children, and taking advantage of the trails in the Colorado mountains.

For more information on Jan, including speaking engagements, please see **janrutherford.com**.

Are you an aspiring Author?

Getting published shouldn't be a dream.

Pylon Publishing LLC specializes in the publication of experienced and aspiring authors alike. The small and knowledgeable company can provide the most custom and specialized services necessary to turn your manuscript into a book quickly. Since Pylon Publishing works directly with the word's largest wholesale book distributor, Ingram Book Company, clients can feel at ease with the widest distribution - Amazon, Barnes and Noble, etc.

It is Pylon Publishing's goal and mission to give authors the most flexibility, distribution, and earnings for their work. As a result, every author retains full control of their book upon publication. That's the Pylon Promise!

Feel free to contact a publishing representative today at pylonpublishing@hotmail.com for a free consultation.

CPSIA information can be obtained at www.ICGtesting.com
Printed in the USA
LVOW06s2058140914

403985LV00002B/2/P